MORETTO: *Portrait of Conte Sciarra Martinengo Cesaresco*. London, National Gallery.

ITALIAN PICTURES OF THE RENAISSANCE

A LIST OF THE PRINCIPAL ARTISTS
AND THEIR WORKS
WITH AN INDEX OF PLACES

BY

BERNARD BERENSON

CENTRAL ITALIAN AND
NORTH ITALIAN SCHOOLS
IN THREE VOLUMES

VOLUME III

PLATES 995–1988

PHAIDON

LISTS OF WORKS BY ITALIAN RENAISSANCE PAINTERS FIRST PUBLISHED IN
1897 (CENTRAL ITALIAN PAINTERS) AND 1907 (NORTH ITALIAN PAINTERS)
REVISED EDITION 1932

NEWLY REVISED AND ILLUSTRATED 1968
ADDITIONAL AND REVISED MATERIAL © PHAIDON PRESS LTD · LONDON 1968

PHAIDON PUBLISHERS INC · NEW YORK
DISTRIBUTORS IN THE UNITED STATES: FREDERICK A. PRAEGER · INC
111 FOURTH AVENUE · NEW YORK · N.Y. 10003
LIBRARY OF CONGRESS CATALOG CARD NUMBER: 68-18905

SBN for complete set of three volumes: 7148 1324 9
SBN for this volume: 7148 1356 7

MADE IN GREAT BRITAIN
TEXT PRINTED BY R. & R. CLARK LTD · EDINBURGH
ILLUSTRATIONS PRINTED BY LONSDALE & BARTHOLOMEW LTD · LEICESTER

CENTRAL ITALIAN AND NORTH ITALIAN
PICTURES OF THE RENAISSANCE

BERENSON'S
ITALIAN PICTURES
OF THE RENAISSANCE

PHAIDON

VOLUME I

TEXT

995. MELOZZO DA FORLÌ: *Inauguration of the Library of Sixtus IV, with the Pope surrounded by Girolamo Riario, Giovanni della Rovere, Platina, Giuliano della Rovere and Raffaele Riario.* Rome, Vatican Pinacoteca. *Not after 1477.*

996. MELOZZO DA FORLÌ AND PALMEZZANO: *Fresco: Angel with the Cross.* Loreto, Santuario. *1484–7.*

997. Melozzo da Forlì (execution by Palmezzano): *Fresco: Entry into Jerusalem*. Loreto, Santuario. *1484–7.*

998. PALMEZZANO: *Fresco: Miracle of S. James at San Domingo de la Calzada.* Forlì, SS. Biagio a Girolamo, Cappella Feo. *Before 1495.* (*Destroyed 1944.*)

999. PALMEZZANO: *Madonna and Child with SS. Sebastian and Roch.* Homeless.

1000. PALMEZZANO: *S. Anthony Abbot enthroned between S. Sebastian and S. John Baptist.* Forlì, Pinacoteca.
Inscribed: Marcus de Melotius. Early work.

1001. PALMEZZANO: *Annunciation*. Forlì, Pinacoteca. *Signed*.

1002. PALMEZZANO: *Madonna and Child with Infant S. John*. Homeless.

1003. PALMEZZANO: *Predella panel: Meeting of Joachim and Anne*. Forlì, S. Mercuriale. *Signed and dated 1510*.

1004. PALMEZZANO: *Holy Family with Infant S. John.*
Phoenix (Arizona), Art Museum. *Signed in Hebrew.*

1005. PALMEZZANO: *Christ carrying the Cross.* Homeless. *Signed.*

1006. PALMEZZANO: *Madonna and Child with Infant S. John and SS. Sebastian and Mary Magdalen.* Homeless. *Signed.*

1007. PALMEZZANO: *Judith.* London, Buckingham Palace, Royal Collection. *Signed and dated 1516.*

1008. SANTI: *Madonna and Child with SS. Thomas Aquinas, Catherine, Anthony Abbot and Thomas, and donor*. Berlin-Ost, Staatliche Museen.

1009. SANTI: *Madonna and Child*. Formerly Berlin, Staatliche Museen. Destroyed 1945.

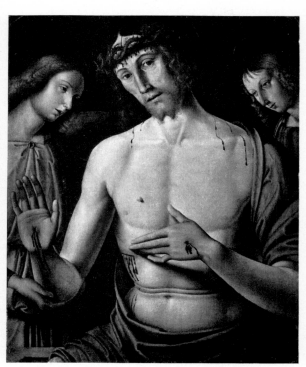

1010. SANTI: *Man of Sorrows*. Budapest, Museum of Fine Arts.

1011. SANTI: *Detail of Madonna and Child: SS. Jerome and Anthony Abbot, and donor.*
Pian di Meleto, Convento di Montefiorentino. *Signed and dated 1489.*

1012. SANTI: *Madonna and Child with SS. John Baptist, Francis, Jerome and Sebastian, and the Buffi family.*
Urbino, Galleria Nazionale delle Marche. *1489.*

1013. SANTI: *Fresco: Madonna and Child with SS. Peter, Francis, Dominic and John Baptist and two Angels.*
Cagli, S. Domenico.

1014. BARTOLOMEO DI GENTILE DA URBINO: *Madonna and Child enthroned.* Lille, Musée des Beaux-Arts.
Signed and dated 1497. 1015. BARTOLOMEO DI GENTILE DA URBINO: *Madonna and Child with S. Catherine
and another female Saint.* Budapest, Museum of Fine Arts. *Signed and dated 1504.*

1016. SANTI: *Detail from Visitation.*
Fano, S. Maria Nuova. *Signed.*

1017. EVANGELISTA DA PIAN DI MELETO ON
SANTI'S DESIGN: *Clio.* Florence, Galleria Corsini.

1018. BETWEEN SANTI AND TIMOTEO VITI: *Shepherd and Nymph.* Florence, Marchese Ginori.

1019. Evangelista da Pian di Meleto on Santi's design: *Erato and Melpomene*.
Florence, Galleria Corsini.

1020. Between Santi and Timoteo Viti: *Shepherd and Nymph*. Florence, Marchese Ginori.

1021. TIBERIO D'ASSISI: *Fresco: S. Francis and his first companions.* Assisi, S. Maria degli Angeli, Cappella del Roseto. *Signed and dated 1506.*

1022. TIBERIO D'ASSISI: *Fresco: Madonna and Child with SS. Michael, Bonaventura, Jerome and Anthony of Padua.* Stroncone, S. Francesco. *Signed and dated 1509.*

1023. TIBERIO D'ASSISI: *Detached fresco: S. Ansanus*. Birmingham, Barber Institute.

1024. TIBERIO D'ASSISI: *Fresco: Tobias and the Angel.*
Castelritaldi, S. Marina. *Signed.*

1025. TIBERIO D'ASSISI: *Detail of fresco: Two Angels.*
Montefalco, Santuario di S. Fortunato.
Signed and dated 1512.

1026. TIBERIO D'ASSISI: *Fresco: The Pardon is announced to the Faithful by S. Francis and the seven Bishops of Umbria.* Assisi, S. Maria degli Angeli. *Dated 1516.*

1027. TIBERIO D'ASSISI: *Fresco: God the Father*. Montefalco, Santuario di S. Fortunato.
Signed and dated 1512.

1028. TIBERIO D'ASSISI: *Fresco: Pope Honorius III grants the requests of S. Francis*. Assisi, S. Maria degli Angeli.
Dated 1516.

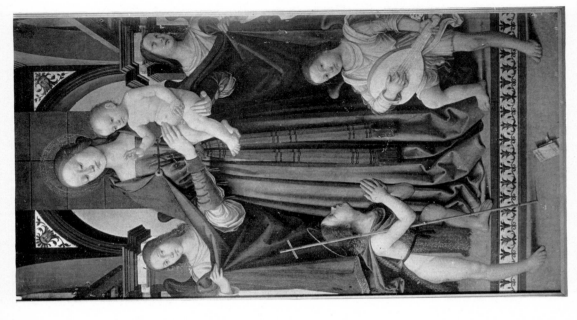

1030. BERTUCCI: *Centre panel of polyptych: Madonna and Child with Infant S. John and Angels. Detail. Faenza, Pinacoteca. Signed and dated 1506.*

1029. BERTUCCI: *Left panel of polyptych: S. Sebastian. Formerly Ferrara, Barbi Cinti Collection.*

1031. BERTUCCI: *Centre panel of polyptych: Adoration of the Magi with donor. Formerly Berlin, Kaiser Friedrich Museum. Destroyed 1945.*

1032. BERTUCCI: *Adoration of the Child with Infant S. John*. Detail. Homeless.

1033. BERNARDINO AND FRANCESCO ZAGANELLI: *Madonna and Child with SS. Francis and Anthony of Padua and another Saint*. Dublin, National Gallery of Ireland. *In the lunette, Dead Christ upheld by Angels*. Rome, Villa Albani. *Signed by both and dated 1509*.

1035. Bernardino Zaganelli: *Madonna and Child enthroned with S. Mary Magdalen and a Bishop Saint. Homeless.*

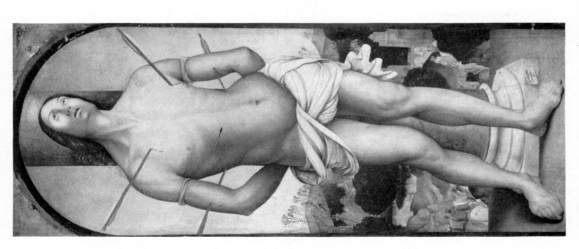

1034. Bernardino Zaganelli: *S. Sebastian. London, National Gallery. Signed and dated 1506.*

1037. BERNARDINO ZAGANELLI: *Madonna and Child with SS. Catherine and Mary Magdalen.* Formerly Vienna, Lederer Collection.

1036. BERNARDINO ZAGANELLI: *Madonna and Child with two female Saints and two Angels.* Oxford, Christ Church.

1038. Bernardino Zaganelli: *Madonna and Child with SS. Sebastian and Roch.*
Formerly New York, Robert Minturn.

1039. Bernardino Zaganelli: *Predella panel: SS. Catherine, Anne with Virgin and Child, and Lucy.*
Baltimore, Walters Art Gallery.

1040. BERNARDINO ZAGANELLI: *Madonna and Child with SS. Agatha and Agnes*. Rome, Galleria Colonna.

1041. BERNARDINO ZAGANELLI: *Lucretia*. Homeless.

1042. BERNARDINO ZAGANELLI: *Penitent Magdalen in the wilderness*. Chambéry, Musée.

1043. FRANCESCO ZAGANELLI: *Annunciation with SS. John Baptist and Anthony of Padua and a donor.*
Formerly Berlin, Kaiser Friedrich Museum, destroyed 1945. *Signed and dated 1509.*

1044–45. Francesco Zaganelli: *Christ carrying the Cross*. Homeless.—*Female Martyr*. Homeless.

1046. Francesco Zaganelli: *Madonna and Child enthroned with SS. Peter and Paul*. Homeless.

1047. Francesco Zaganelli: *Immaculate Conception*. Forlì, Pinacoteca. *Signed and dated 1513.*

1048. BERNARDINO AND FRANCESCO ZAGANELLI: *Madonna and Child enthroned with SS. Apollinaris and Christopher*. Detail. Castel di Mezzo, Parish Church.

1049 FRANCESCO ZAGANELLI:
S. Sebastian. Ferrara, Pinacoteca.
Signed and dated 1513.

1050. FRANCESCO ZAGANELLI: *Dead Christ upheld by Angels*.
Formerly Rome, Marchese Patrizi.

1051. FRANCESCO ZAGANELLI: *Altarpiece: Baptism of Christ; in lunette, Dead Christ upheld by Angels.*
London, National Gallery. *Signed and dated 1514.*

1052. Francesco Zaganelli: *Christ carrying the Cross.* Naples, Museo Nazionale. 1053. Francesco Zaganelli: *Holy Family with female martyr.* Homeless. *Signed and dated 1514.*

1054–5. FRANCESCO ZAGANELLI: *Fragments of polyptych: Rolando Pallavicini and his daughter; Domicilla Gambara Pallavicini. Parma, SS. Annunziata. Commissioned 1518.*

1056. Francesco Zaganelli: *Mystic Marriage of S. Catherine*. Ravenna, Seminario.

1057. VITI: *Noli me tangere, with SS. Michael and Anthony Abbot. Cagli, S. Angelo. Signed. 1518–19.*

COMICA LASCIVO GAVDET SERMONE THALIA   246

1058. VITI: *Thalia.* Florence, Galleria Corsini.

1059. Viti: *S. Apollonia*. Urbino, Galleria Nazionale delle Marche.

1060. VITI: *Stained glass window: Annunciation and Putti*. Urbino, Galleria Nazionale delle Marche.

1061. VITI: *S. Mary Magdalen*. Gubbio, Duomo. *Signed and dated 1521.*

1062. PERUGINO: *Madonna and blessing Child.*
Paris, Musée Jacquemart-André. *Early work.*

1063. PINTURICCHIO: *Madonna and Child standing
on parapet.* London, National Gallery. *Early work.*

1064. ANTONIAZZO ROMANO: *Madonna holding Child
on parapet and two Cherubim.* Los Angeles,
Museum of Art, Simon Foundation.

1065. MASTER OF THE GARDNER ANNUNCIATION:
Madonna adoring the Child. Baltimore,
Walters Art Gallery.

1066. FIORENZO DI LORENZO: *Madonna and Child with S. Jerome*. Boston, Museum of Fine Arts.

1067. Fiorenzo di Lorenzo: *Madonna and Child enthroned with SS. Christopher and Sebastian.*
Frankfurt, Staedel Institute.

1068. Perugino: *Fresco: S. Sebastian.* Detail.
Cerqueto, Parish Church. *Signed and dated 1478.*

1069. Fiorenzo di Lorenzo: *S. Sebastian.*
Rome, Palazzo Spada.

MARIA · XGO · PRIS · MR · 7 GE · M · CCCDOXXI

1070. MASTER OF THE GARDNER ANNUNCIATION: *Madonna of the pomegranate*.
Berlin-Ost, Staatliche Museen. *Dated 1481.*

1071. MASTER OF THE GARDNER ANNUNCIATION: *Lunette: Blessing Redeemer and two Angels.*
Barcelona, Capuchin Church de Sarrià.

1072. MASTER OF THE GARDNER ANNUNCIATION: *Annunciation; in predella, Dead Christ and SS. Peter and Paul.* Boston, Isabella Stewart Gardner Museum.

1073. PIER MATTEO D'AMELIA: *Madonna and Child with SS. John Baptist and Francis; in lunette, God the Father blessing and two Angels.* Amelia, Museo Civico.

1074. FIORENZO DI LORENZO: Triptych: Madonna and Child enthroned with two Angels, kneeling Flagellant and Prior; SS. Mustiola and Andrew; SS. Peter and Francis; in predella, Dead Christ in sepulchre with mourning Virgin and S. John Evangelist, adored by two Confratelli della Giustizia; SS. Bernardino and John Baptist; SS. Jerome and Sebastian. Perugia, Galleria Nazionale dell'Umbria.

1075. FIORENZO DI LORENZO: *Detached fresco:*
Madonna of Mercy. Perugia, Galleria Nazionale dell'Umbria.
Formerly signed and dated 1476.

1076. FIORENZO DI LORENZO: *Altarpiece with niche for missing sculpture:*
Madonna and Child with Angels and Putti; below, SS. Peter and Paul.
Perugia, Galleria Nazionale dell'Umbria. Signed and dated 1487.

1077. SCACCO: *Madonna and Child enthroned*. Fragment.
London, Mrs. Lloyd Griscom.

1078. SCACCO: *Detail from the triptych of the Annunciation*. Fondi, S. Pietro. *Signed and dated 1499.*

1079. SCACCO: *Right panel of triptych: SS. John Evangelist and (?)Romuald.*
Naples, Museo Nazionale. *Signed and dated 1493.*

1080. SCACCO: *Detail of triptych: Coronation of the Virgin*. Naples, Museo Nazionale.

1081. SCACCO: *Dead Christ with mourning Virgin and S. John Evangelist*. Homeless.

1082. SCACCO: *S. Michael*. Salerno, S. Pietro in Vincoli.

1083. Lorenzo da Viterbo: *Detail of fresco of the Assumption of the Virgin*. Viterbo, S. Maria della Verità. 1469.

1084. LORENZO DA VITERBO: *Frescoed vault: The Evangelists, the Fathers of the Church, Prophets and Doctors of the Church.* Viterbo, S. Maria della Verità. *1469.*

1085. Lorenzo da Viterbo: *Altarpiece: Madonna and Child enthroned with SS. Michael and Peter.*
Rome, Galleria Nazionale, Palazzo Barberini. *Signed and dated 1472.*

1086. Lorenzo da Viterbo: *Predella panel: Adoration of the Magi. Detail.* Bayeux, Musée.

1087. Antoniazzo Romano: *Centre panel of triptych: Madonna suckling the Child,
with donor. Rieti, Museo Civico. Signed and dated 1464.*

1088. ANTONIAZZO ROMANO: *Triptych: Madonna and Child, S. Francis, S. Anthony of Padua. Subiaco, S. Francesco. Signed and dated 1467.*

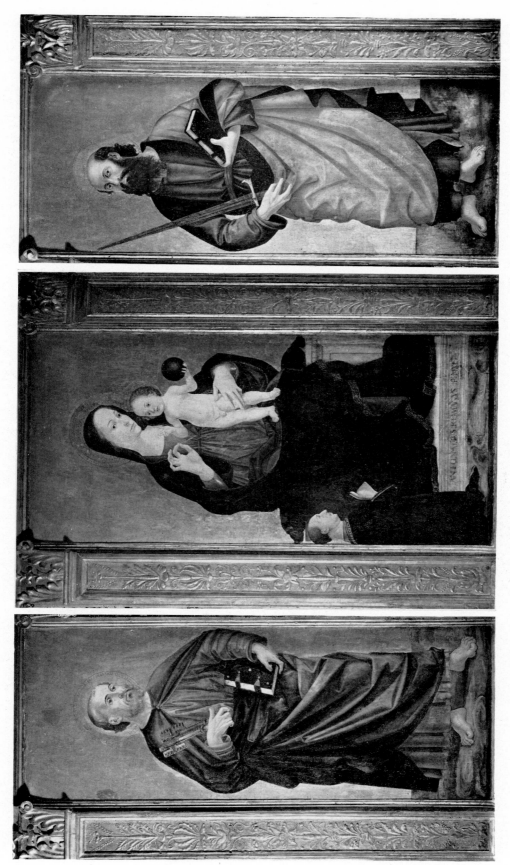

1089. ANTONIAZZO ROMANO: *Triptych: Madonna and Child enthroned with donor, S. Peter, S. Paul,* Fondi, S. Pietro. *Signed.*

1090. ANTONIAZZO ROMANO: *Detail of fresco of the Assumption. Tivoli, S. Giovanni Evangelista.*

1091. ANTONIAZZO ROMANO: *Detail of fresco of the Birth of S. John Baptist. Tivoli, S. Giovanni Evangelista.*

1092. ANTONIAZZO ROMANO: *Dominican Saint with the Redeemer and a worshipper.*
Rome, S. Sabina.

1093. ANTONIAZZO ROMANO: *Virgin and Infant S. John adoring the Child*. Detail. Homeless.

1094. ANTONIAZZO ROMANO: *Annunciation with Dominican Cardinal Juan de Torquemada recommending three poor girls to the Virgin*. Rome, S. Maria sopra Minerva.

1095. PERUGINO: *Adoration of the Magi*. Perugia, Galleria Nazionale dell'Umbria. *Before 1478.*

1096. PERUGINO: *Christ on the Cross with SS. Jerome and Francis, Blessed Giovanni Colombini,*
SS. John Baptist and Mary Magdalen. Florence, Uffizi. *Early work.*

1097. PERUGINO: *Triptych: Crucifixion, S. Jerome, S. Mary Magdalen.* Washington, National Gallery of Art, Mellon Collection.

1098. PERUGINO: *Polyptych: Nativity and two Angels, SS. Michael and John Baptist, SS. Jerome and George; above, Crucifixion, Angel and Virgin of the Annunciation. Rome, Villa Albani. Signed and dated* 14(91?).

1099. PERUGINO: *Nicodemus. Detail from Dead Christ
in Sepulchre*. Williamstown, Mass., Clark Art Institute.

1100. PERUGINO: *Bust of a young man*.
Leningrad, Hermitage.

1101. PERUGINO: *S. Augustine enthroned and kneeling members of a Confraternity*.
Pittsburgh, Carnegie Institute.

1102. PERUGINO: *Baptism of Christ*. Vienna, Kunsthistorisches Museum.

1103. PERUGINO: *Detached fresco from S. Pier Maggiore: Dead Christ on Tomb.*
Formerly Florence, Palazzo Albizzi.

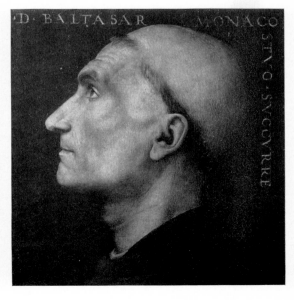

1104–5. PERUGINO: *Heads of Don Biagio Milanesi and Don Baldassarre of the Vallombrosan Order.*
Florence, Uffizi. *1500.*

1106. PERUGINO: *Frescoed decoration*. Perugia, Collegio del Cambio.

1107. PERUGINO: *Combat of Love and Chastity*. Detail. Paris, Louvre. *1505.*

1108. PERUGINO: *Detail of frescoed vault: Christ between S. John Baptist and Satan.* Rome, Vatican,
Stanza dell'Incendio. *1507–8.*

1109. LO SPAGNA: *Coronation of the Virgin with Angels, Prophets, Sibyls and Saints; in pilasters, six small Saints*. Todi, Pinacoteca. *Dated 1511.*

1110. Lo Spagna: *Madonna and Child enthroned with two Angels, SS. Catherine, Francis, Clare and Louis and two other Saints.* Assisi, S. Francesco. *Dated 1516.*

1111. LO SPAGNA: *Detached fresco: Madonna and Child with SS. Jerome, Nicholas of Tolentino, Catherine and Brizio.* Spoleto, Palazzo Comunale. *1514–16.*

1112. LO SPAGNA: *Fresco: S. Michael appears on Mount Gargano.* Gavelli, S. Michele Arcangelo. *Signed and dated 1518.*

1113. PASTURA: *Detached fresco: Two Angels and two Cherubim* round a Madonna by Andrea di Giovanni. Viterbo, Museo Civico.

1114. PASTURA: *Madonna and Child.* Homeless.

1115. PASTURA: *Madonna and Child crowned by Cherubim.* Tuscania, S. Maria del Riposo.

1116. PASTURA: *Madonna and Child with SS. Jerome and Francis.* Formerly Paris, M. F. Gentili.

1117. PASTURA: *Nativity with SS. John Baptist and Bartholomew*. Viterbo, Museo Civico.

1118. PASTURA: *Fresco: Music.* Rome, Vatican, Appartamenti Borgia. *1492–4.*

1120. PASTURA: *Detail of fresco: Virgin of the Annunciation. Orvieto, S. Maria Assunta. 1498.*

1119. PASTURA: *Fresco: Madonna and blessing Child. Viterbo, Palazzo Chigi.*

1121. PASTURA: *Fresco: Marriage of the Virgin.* Tarquinia, Duomo. *1508–9.*

1122. PINTURICCHIO: *Fresco in lunette: Madonna and Child with Angels and Cherubim.* Perugia, Municipio. *14(86?).*

1123–4. PINTURICCHIO: *Miniatures: Porta S. Angelo Auguste Perusie.* Vienna, Akademie. *1485.*—*Porta Solis Auguste Perusie.* Formerly Perugia, Palazzo Graziani. *Dated 1486.*

1125. PINTURICCHIO: *Detail of fresco: S. Bernardino in penitence at Porta Tufi near Siena.*
Rome, S. Maria in Araceli, Cappella Bufalini.

1126. PINTURICCHIO: *Fresco: Episode from the myth of Apis*. Rome, Vatican, Borgia Apartments. Sala dei Santi. *1492–5*.

1127. PINTURICCHIO: *Detail from the fresco of the Resurrection: Pope Alexander VI*. Rome, Vatican, Borgia Apartments, Sala dei Misteri. *1492–5*.

1128. PINTURICCHIO: *Portrait of a boy*. Dresden, Gallery.

1129. PINTURICCHIO: *Fresco: Episode from the myth of Isis and Osiris*. Rome, Vatican, Borgia Apartments, Sala dei Santi. *1492–5*.

1130. PINTURICCHIO: *S. Bartholomew*. Formerly Lyons, M. E. Aynard.

1131. PINTURICCHIO: *Detail from predella of polyptych: S. Augustine and the child who wanted to empty the sea; two Evangelists*. Perugia, Galleria Nazionale dell'Umbria. *1495.*

1132–3. Pinturicchio: *Details of polyptych: S. Augustine and S. Jerome; above, Angel and Virgin of the Annunciation.* Perugia, Galleria Nazionale dell'Umbria. *1495.*

1134. PINTURICCHIO: *Fresco: Adoration of the Shepherds*. Detail. Spello, Collegiata di S. Maria. *Signed and dated 1501.*

1135. PINTURICCHIO: *Fresco: Adoration of the Shepherds*. Detail. Spello, Collegiata di S. Maria. *Signed and dated 1501.*

1136. PINTURICCHIO: *Fresco: Annunciation*. Detail. Spello, Collegiata di S. Maria. *Signed and dated 1501.*

1137. PINTURICCHIO: *Fresco: Self-portrait*. Detail from the Annunciation.
Spello, Collegiata di S. Maria. *Signed and dated 1501.*

1138. PINTURICCHIO: *Fresco: Christ among the Doctors*. Detail. Spello, Collegiata di S. Maria.
Signed and dated 1501.

1139. PINTURICCHIO: *Fresco: Christ among the Doctors.* Detail. Spello, Collegiata di S. Maria.
Signed and dated 1501.

1140. PINTURICCHIO: *Fresco: Christ among the Doctors.* Detail. Spello, Collegiata di S. Maria.
Signed and dated 1501.

1141. PINTURICCHIO: *Fresco: Enea Silvio Piccolomini as ambassador before the King of Scotland.*
Siena, S. Maria Assunta, Libreria Piccolomini. *1503–8.*

1142. PINTURICCHIO: *Fresco: Pope Pius II arriving at Ancona just before his death*. Siena, S. Maria Assunta, Libreria Piccolomini. *1503–8*.

1143. PINTURICCHIO: *Miniature: Christ on the Cross with the Virgin and S. John Evangelist.*
Rome, Vatican, Biblioteca.

1144. PINTURICCHIO: *Way to Calvary*. Isolabella, Palazzo Borromeo. *Signed and dated 1513.*

1145. PINTURICCHIO AND ASSISTANTS: *Detached frescoed ceiling: Putti with garlands, Rape of Proserpine;*
Chariot of Apollo; Triumph of Mars; Chariot of Ceres; Triumph of Cybele; Triumph of Alexander;
Triumph of Amphitrite; Triumph of a warrior; in ovals and semiovals, Galatea; Hunt of the Calydonian boar;
Judgement of Paris; Helle on a ram; Hercules and Omphale; Rape of Europa; in roundels, Bacchus,
Pan and Silenus; Jupiter and Antiope; The Three Graces; Venus and Cupid.
New York, Metropolitan Museum.

1146. BALDUCCI: *Ceiling frescoes: Mythological and allegorical scenes.* Siena, S. Maria Assunta, Libreria Piccolomini.

1147. BALDUCCI: *Madonna of the Assumption with S. Francis and S. Catherine of Siena.* Siena, S. Spirito. *Predella: S. Francis receiving stigmata, Pietà, S. Catherine of Siena receiving stigmata.* Siena, Pinacoteca.

1148. BALDUCCI (on Pinturicchio's cartoon): *Nativity*. Siena, Pinacoteca.

1149. BALDUCCI: *Predella panel: Crucifixion*. Castle Ashby, Marquess of Northampton.

1150. BALDUCCI: *Predella panel: Adoration of the Magi*. Detail. Versailles, James H. Hyde.

1151. BALDUCCI: *Triumph of Bacchus*. Detail. Gubbio, Palazzo dei Consoli.

1152. BALDUCCI: *Apollo and a Muse*.
Formerly Florence, Loeser Collection.

1153. BALDUCCI: *Triumph of Bacchus*. Detail.
Gubbio, Palazzo dei Consoli.

1154. EUSEBIO DA SAN GIORGIO: *S. Sebastian*. Homeless.

1155. EUSEBIO DA SAN GIORGIO: *Adoration of the Magi*. Detail. Perugia, Galleria Nazionale dell'Umbria.
Dated 1505.

1156. Eusebio da San Giorgio: *Adoration of the Magi*. Perugia, S. Pietro. Dated 1508.

1157. Eusebio da San Giorgio: *Madonna and Child enthroned with SS. Anthony of Padua, John Evangelist, Andrew and Nicholas of Tolentino*. Matelica, S. Francesco. *Signed and dated 1512.*

1158. EUSEBIO DA SAN GIORGIO: *Predella panel: S. Nicholas of Tolentino saves two hanged men.*
Formerly Rome, Schiff Collection.

1159–60. EUSEBIO DA SAN GIORGIO: *Two predella panels: S. Nicholas of Tolentino saves a youth from drowning; and resuscitates the birds.* Detroit, Art Institute.

1161. FRANCESCO DA TOLENTINO: *Fresco: Madonna and Child with SS. Catervo and Sebastian.*
Tolentino, Duomo.

1162. FRANCESCO DA TOLENTINO: *Fresco: Adoration of the Magi.* Naples, S. Maria Nuova.

1163. Francesco da Tolentino: *Lunette of polyptych: Crucifixion*. Liveri di Nola. Santuario di S. Maria. *Signed and dated 1530 or 1531.*

1164–5. Francesco da Tolentino: *Details of polyptych: S. Barbara; S. Anthony Abbot*. Liveri di Nola, Santuario di S. Maria. *Signed and dated 1530 or 1531.*

1166. COLA D'AMATRICE: *Detail of polyptych: Pietà.*
Ascoli Piceno, Pinacoteca. *1509.*

1167. COLA D'AMATRICE: *SS. Ursula, Mary Magdalen, Catherine and John Baptist.* Detail.
Campli, Parish Church.

1168. COLA D'AMATRICE: *Madonna and Child enthroned with SS. Peter, Louis of Toulouse and Francis.*
Homeless. *Signed and dated 1512.*

1169. COLA D'AMATRICE: *Side-panel of triptych: SS. Benedict and Lawrence.*
Rome, Vatican Pinacoteca.

1170. COLA D'AMATRICE: *Side-panel of triptych: SS. Mary Magdalen and Gertrude.*
Rome, Vatican, Pinacoteca.

1171. COLA D'AMATRICE: *Madonna and Child with four Saints; in background, Angels fighting devils over Ascoli.*
Detail. Ascoli, S. Vittore. *Dated 1514.*

1172. COLA D'AMATRICE: *Mourning over the dead Christ*. Homeless.

1173. COLA D'AMATRICE: *Christ on the way to Calvary*. Detail. Ascoli Piceno, Pinacoteca.

1174. Raphael: *Madonna and Child.* Homeless.

1175. Raphael: *Predella panel: S. Jerome saves Bishop Silvanus from being beheaded and inflicts that death on Sabinianus.* Raleigh, N.C., Museum of Art.

1176. RAPHAEL: *Coronation of the Virgin*. Detail. Rome, Vatican, Pinacoteca. *1503*.

1177. RAPHAEL: *Madonna del Prato*. Vienna, Kunsthistorisches Museum. *Dated 1505.*

1178. RAPHAEL: *The young warrior's dream*. London, National Gallery. *Early work.*

1179. RAPHAEL: *Predella panel: Charity(?) and two putti*. Rome, Vatican, Pinacoteca. *1507.*

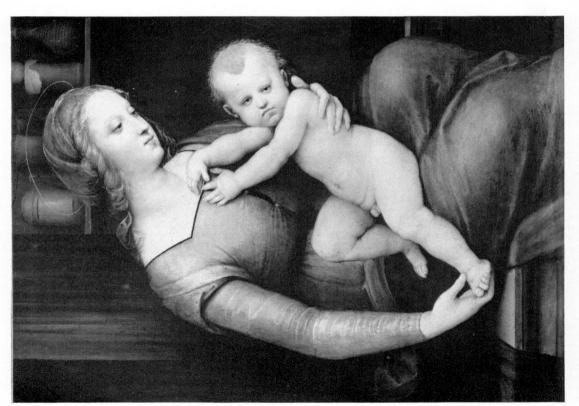

1183. RAPHAEL: 'Niccolini Cowper' Madonna. Washington,
National Gallery of Art, Mellon Collection. *Dated 1508.*

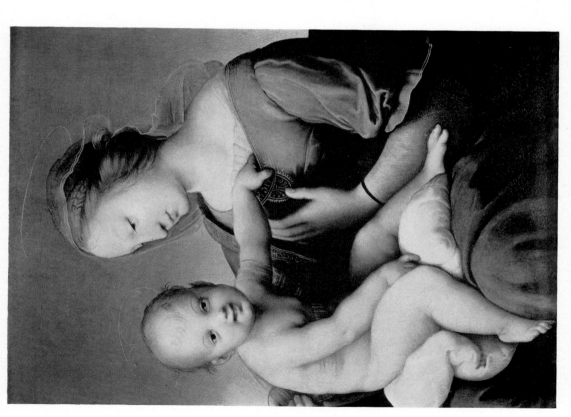

1182. RAPHAEL: 'Bridgewater' Madonna. Edinburgh, National Gallery
of Scotland, on loan from the Duke of Sutherland.

1184. SALA DI GALATEA. Rome, Villa Farnesina. Ceiling frescoes by Peruzzi, lunettes by Sebastiano del Piombo, fresco of *Triumph of Galatea* by Raphael. 1511.

1185. STANZA DELLA SEGNATURA. Rome, Palazzo Vaticano. Frescoes of *Parnassus* and *School of Athens* by Raphael (1509–11); monochrome scenes in dado by Perino del Vaga (c. 1542).

1186. RAPHAEL: *Madonna di Foligno with SS. John Baptist, Francis and Jerome recommending Sigismondo de' Conti. Vatican, Pinacoteca. 1511–12.*

1187. RAPHAEL: *Ceiling mosaic on his design: The Eternal and planets guided by Angels.*
Rome, S. Maria del Popolo, Cappella Chigi. *Finished 1516.*

1188. RAPHAEL: *Fresco: Four Sibyls and Angels*. Rome, S. Maria della Pace. *About 1514.*

1189. RAPHAEL: *Tapestry cartoon: Christ giving the keys to S. Peter*. London, Victoria and Albert Museum. *Late work.*

The inscription on the base reads:
RGIVS PAVLLVS
IAE PROCOS:
ISTIANAM FIDEM
MPLECTITVR·
PREDICATIONE

1190. RAPHAEL: *Detail of tapestry cartoon: Elymas struck with blindness.* London, Victoria and Albert Museum.
Late work.

1191. FOPPA: *Detached fresco: The young Cicero*. London, Wallace Colletion.

1192. FOPPA: *Crucifixion*. Bergamo, Accademia Carrara. *Signed and dated 1456.*

1193. FOPPA: *Detached fresco: Madonna and Child with SS. John Baptist and John Evangelist*. Milan, Brera.
Dated 1485.

1194. FOPPA: *Detail of Madonna and Child with four Angels*. Milan, Brera.

1195. FOPPA: *Detail of Adoration of the Magi*. London, National Gallery. *Late work*.

1196. FOPPA: *Centre panel of polyptych: Madonna and Child enthroned with Angels and Cardinal Giuliano della Rovere as donor.* Savona, S. Maria di Castello. *Signed and dated 1490.*

1197. Brea: *Side-panel of Della Rovere polyptych: S. John Evangelist.* Savona, S. Maria di Castello.
Signed and dated 1490.

1198. BREA: *Triptych: Pietà, S. Martin with the beggar, S. Catherine.* Nice-Cimiez, Church of Franciscan Monastery. *Signed and dated 1475.*

1199–1201. BREA: *Detail of polyptych: S. Catherine of Siena flanked by SS. Lucy and Agatha.* Taggia, S. Domenico. *1488.*

1202. BREA: *Centre panel of polyptych: Madonna of Mercy.*
Taggia, S. Domenico. *1483–4.*

1203. BREA: *Centre panel of polyptych: Baptism of Christ with kneeling Benedetto and Lazzaro Curli.*
Taggia, S. Domenico. *Formerly dated 1495.*

1204. BREA: *Madonna and Child enthroned*. Detail. Homeless.

1205. BREA: *Detail of predella: S. Margaret meets Olibrius and is arrested*. Nice, Musée Masséna.

1206. BREA: *Madonna crowned by Angels and blessing Child*. Homeless.

1207. BREA: *Predella panel: Visitation*. New Haven, Yale University Art Gallery.

1208. BREA: *Polyptych: Annunciation, S. Louis of Toulouse, S. Anthony Abbot; in upper register, Crucifixion flanked by SS. Christopher, John Baptist, Raphael with Tobias, Sebastian, Michael and Catherine; in predella, Christ and the Apostles.* Lieuche, Parish Church. *Dated 1499.*

1209. BREA: *Coronation of the Virgin, All Saints; in predella, Mourning over the dead Christ.*
Genoa, S. Maria di Castello. *Commissioned 1512.*

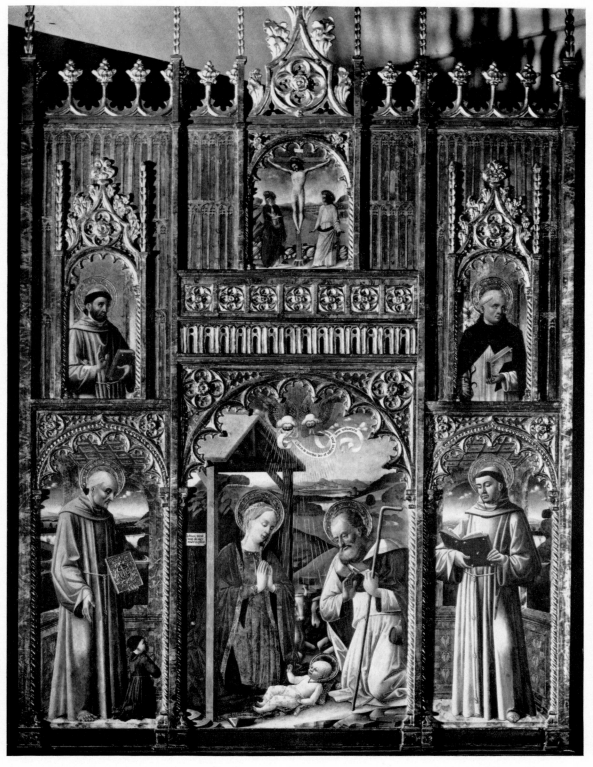

1210. MASSONE: *Polyptych: Nativity, S. Bernardino with donor, S. Bonaventura; in upper register, S. Francis, Crucifixion, S. Dominic.* Savona, Pinacoteca. *Signed. About 1490–5.*

1211. MASSONE: *SS. Catherine and John Baptist.* Detail.
Liverpool, Walker Art Gallery.

1212. MASSONE: *Detail of polyptych: Annunciation.* Genoa, S. Maria di Castello. *Probably about 1463.*

1213. MASSONE: *Crucifixion*. Savona, Pinacoteca.

1214. MASSONE: *Side-panel of polyptych: S. Francis recommending Pope Sixtus IV.*
Paris, Louvre. *1490.*

1215. MASSONE: *Centre panel of polyptych: Nativity.* Paris, Louvre.
Signed and dated 1490.

1216. SPANZOTTI: *Triptych: Madonna and Child enthroned, S. Ubaldus, S. Sebastian. Turin, Galleria Sabauda. Signed.*

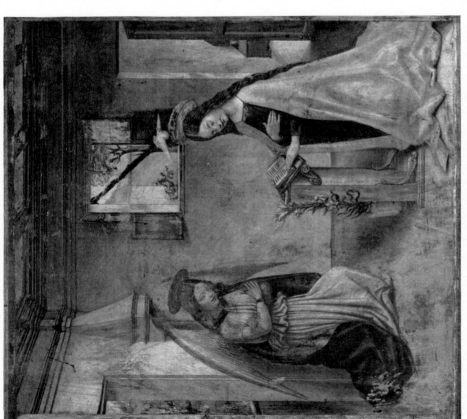

1217–18. SPANZOTTI: *Frescoes: Annunciation; Flight into Egypt. Ivrea, S. Bernardino. About 1485–95.*

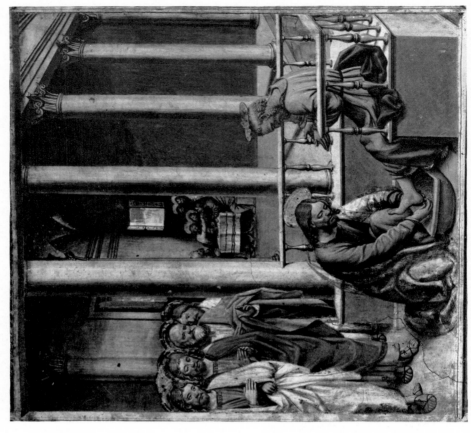

1219–20. SPANZOTTI: *Frescoes: Christ among the Doctors; Washing of Feet*. Ivrea, S. Bernardino. *About 1485–95*.

1222. DEFENDENTE FERRARI: *Christ and the Doctors*. Detail. Later version of Spanzotti, Fig. 1221. Stuttgart, Landesgalerie. *Signed and dated 1526.*

1221. SPANZOTTI: *Christ and the Doctors*. Turin, Museo Civico. *Signed. Before 1513.*

1223. SPANZOTTI: *Landing of S. Mary Magdalen at Marseilles.*
Turin, Museo Civico. *Before 1513.*

1224. SPANZOTTI: *Baptism of Christ*. Turin, S. Giovanni Battista. *1508–10*.

1225. SPANZOTTI(?): *Birth of SS. Crispinus and Crispinianus; they receive their mother's blessing; they worship at an altar.* Turin, S. Giovanni Battista.

1226. SPANZOTTI(?): *SS. Crispinus and Crispinianus are tied round a tree and tortured with burning irons; they are scourged and skinned; they are thrown into a river.* Turin, S. Giovanni Battista.

1227. Spanzotti(?): *SS. Crispinus and Crispinianus making and selling shoes.*
Turin, S. Giovanni Battista.

1229. MACRINO D'ALBA: *Pietà*. Homeless.

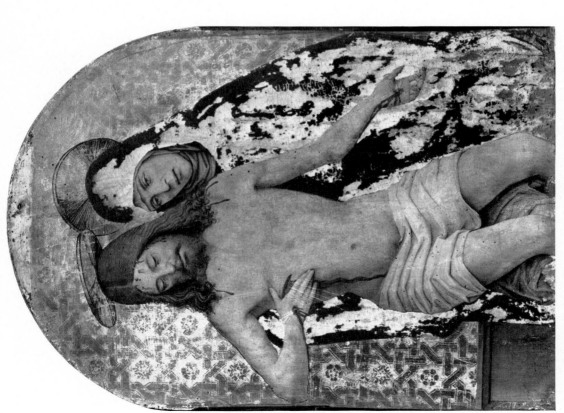

1228. SPANZOTTI: *Pietà*. Budapest, Museum of Fine Arts.

1230. MACRINO D'ALBA: *Triptych: Madonna and Child enthroned; SS. James and John Evangelist with male donor; SS. John Baptist and Dominic with female donor. Turin, Museo Civico. Signed and dated 1494.*

1231. MACRINO D'ALBA: *Madonna and Child in glory with six Angels and SS. John Baptist, James, Bishop Ugo and penitent Jerome.* Turin, Galleria Sabauda. *Signed and dated 1498.*

1232. MACRINO D'ALBA: *Nativity with SS. John Baptist, Jerome, and George, and donor; in the background the Colosseum*. New York, Historical Society. *Signed and dated 1505.*

1233. MACRINO D'ALBA: *Madonna suckling the Child, and two Angels*. Homeless.

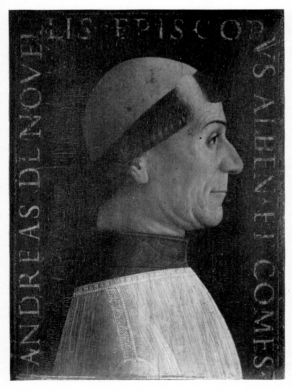

1234. MACRINO D'ALBA: *Bishop Andrea de' Novelli*.
Milan, Borromeo Collection.

1235. MACRINO D'ALBA: *A Knight of Malta*. New York,
Pierpont Morgan Library. *Signed and dated 1499*.

1236. MACRINO D'ALBA: *S. Francis receiving stigmata, with portrait of Enrico Balistrero.*
Turin, Galleria Sabauda. *Formerly signed and dated 1506.*

1237. SPANZOTTI: *Fresco: Adoration of the Child*. Detail. Rivarolo Canavese, S. Francesco.

1238. DEFENDENTE FERRARI: *Adoration of the Child*. Detail. Susa, S. Giusto.

1239. MACRINO D'ALBA: *Detail of Madonna and Child with Saints and donors*. Alba, Palazzo Comunale. *Signed and dated 1501*.

1240. LANINO: *Fresco from S. Marta: Three music-making putti*. Milan, Brera.

1241. Spanzotti (assisted by Defendente): *Assumption*. Budapest,
Museum of Fine Arts. *Dated 1500.*

1242. DEFENDENTE FERRARI: *Centre panel of polyptych: Assumption.*
Vercelli, Museo Borgogna.

1243. DEFENDENTE FERRARI: *Madonna and Child enthroned*. Detail. Caselle Torinese, Municipio. *Dated 1501*.

1244. DEFENDENTE FERRARI: *Predella panel: Circumcision.* Turin, Museo Civico.

1245. DEFENDENTE FERRARI: *Predella panel: Naming of S. John Baptist.* Formerly Budapest, Sandor Lederer.

1246. DEFENDENTE FERRARI: *Predella panel: Vision of S. Bernard.* Avigliana, S. Giovanni.

1248. Defendente Ferrari: *S. Jerome praying in the wilderness.* Turin, Museo Civico. Dated 1520.

1247. Defendente Ferrari: *Nativity by night.* Turin, Museo Civico. Dated 1510.

1249–50. DEFENDENTE FERRARI: *Flagellation; Christ seated on the Cross.* Bergamo, Accademia Carrara.

1251. DEFENDENTE FERRARI: *Adoration of the Child, with Blessed Vermondus recommending donor.*
Ivrea, Duomo. *Signed and dated 1521.*

1252. DEFENDENTE FERRARI: *Madonna and Child with S. Anne and two music-making Angels.*
Amsterdam, Rijksmuseum. *Signed and dated 1528.*

1253. DEFENDENTE FERRARI: *Portable triptych: Adoration of the Magi, Nativity, Pietà. Stresa Borromeo, Istituto Rosmini. Signed and dated 1523.*

1255. DEFENDENTE FERRARI: *Panel of polyptych:*
S. Jerome reading. Homeless.

1254. DEFENDENTE FERRARI: SS. *Sebastian and Roch.* Detail.
Avigliana, S. Giovanni.

1256. DEFENDENTE FERRARI: *Adoration of the Shepherds*. Bergamo, Accademia Carrara. *Signed.*

1257. DEFENDENTE FERRARI: *Predella panels: Judgement and Beheading of S. Tiburtius*.
San Benigno Canavese, Assunta.

1258. **DEFENDENTE FERRARI:** *Polyptych: Nativity; SS. Anthony Abbot and Roch; SS. Sebastian and Bernardino of Siena; in predella, Life of S. Anthony Abbot.* Buttigliera Alta, S. Antonio di Ranverso.

1259. GIROLAMO GIOVENONE (AFTER DEFENDENTE): *Adoration of the Child; in predella, Man of Sorrows, S. Roch and S. Sebastian*. Vercelli, Museo Borgogna.

1260. GIROLAMO GIOVENONE: *Madonna and Child enthroned, with SS. Abbondius and Dominic recommending the widow of Domenico Buronzo and her children.* Turin, Galleria Sabauda. *Signed and dated 1514.*

1261. GIROLAMO GIOVENONE: *Triptych: Madonna and Child, four Saints, donor and his wife.*
Bergamo, Accademia Carrara. *Signed and dated 1527.*

1262. GIROLAMO GIOVENONE: *Two panels of polyptych: S. John Baptist with kneeling monk;*
S. Christopher. Vercelli, Museo Borgogna.

1263. Girolamo Giovenone: *Adoration of the Child with SS. Joseph, Peter Martyr, Anthony Abbot and Anthony of Padua.* Vercelli, S. Cristoforo. *Late work.*

1264. GIROLAMO GIOVENONE: *S. Ambrose*. Vercelli, S. Francesco.
1527–35.

1265. GAUDENZIO FERRARI: *Panel of polyptych: Expulsion of Joachim*. Turin, Galleria Sabauda. (*1508?*).

1266. GAUDENZIO FERRARI: *Life of Christ. Varallo Sesia, S. Maria delle Grazie. Signed and dated 1513.*

1267–8. GAUDENZIO FERRARI: Frescoes: *Betrayal of Christ*; *Nailing to the Cross*. Details from Plate 1266. Varallo Sesia, S. Maria delle Grazie. *1513*.

1269. Gaudenzio Ferrari: *Detail of fresco and painted statuary: Crucifixion*. Varallo Sesia, Sacro Monte. *1523*.

1270. GAUDENZIO FERRARI: *Crucifixion*. Turin, Galleria Sabauda.

1271. Gaudenzio Ferrari (assisted by Lanino): *Fresco: Adoration of the Shepherds.*
Vercelli, S. Cristoforo. *1532–4.*

1272. GAUDENZIO FERRARI (ASSISTED BY LANINO): *Fresco: Adoration of the Magi*. Vercelli, S Cristoforo.
1532–4.

1273. GAUDENZIO FERRARI: *Detail of fresco: Concert of Angels*. Saronno, S. Maria dei Miracoli. *1534–6*.

1274. Gaudenzio Ferrari: *Flight into Egypt*. Como, Duomo. *Late work*.

1275. LANINO: *Assumption; in predella, Life of the Virgin*. Biella, S. Sebastiano. *Signed and dated 1543.*

1276. LANINO: *Frescoes: Beheading of S. George; in lunette, Trial by fire.* Milan, S. Ambrogio.
Signed. About 1545–50.

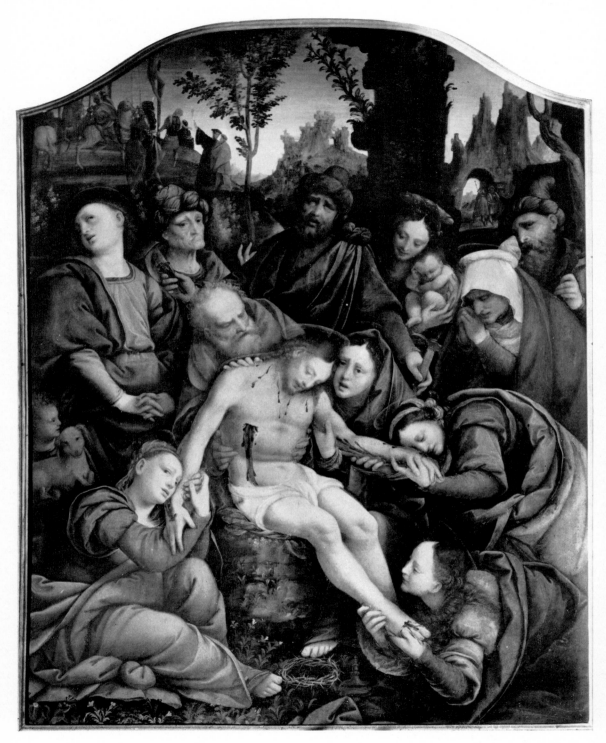

1277. LANINO: *Deposition*. Vercelli, S. Giuliano. *Signed and dated 1547.*

1278. LANINO: *Deposition*. Turin, Galleria Sabauda. *Signed and dated 1558.*

1279. LANINO: *Madonna and Child enthroned with six Dominican Saints and eight donors.*
Raleigh, North Carolina Museum of Art, Kress Collection. *Signed and dated 1552.*

1280. LANINO: *Madonna and Child with SS. John Baptist, Augustine, Lucy and James.*
Turin, Galleria Sabauda. *Signed and dated 1564.*

1281. LANINO: *Portrait of Cassiano dal Pozzo*. Rome, Pinacoteca Capitolina. *Signed.*

1282. LANINO: *Detail from the Adoration of the Magi.*
Vercelli, S. Giuliano.

1283. LANINO: *Detail from Madonna and Child with Saints.*
Turin, Galleria Sabauda. *Signed.*

1284. LANINO: *Detail from Madonna with SS. Francis and
Bernardino.* Vercelli, Museo Borgogna. *Signed and dated 1563.*

1285. FRANCESCO DAI LIBRI: *Triptych: Madonna and Child with donor; S. Maria Consolatrice; S. Catherine of Alexandria; in predella, the four Church Fathers and scenes from the life of S. Maria Consolatrice.* Verona, Museo di Castelvecchio.

1286. FRANCESCO DAI LIBRI: Triptych: *Dead Christ with the Symbols of the Passion; S. Benedict; S. Albert.* Verona, SS. Nazaro e Celso.

1287. FRANCESCO DAI LIBRI: *Triptych: S. Cecilia, S. Tiburtius and S. Valerian.* Verona, Museo di Castelvecchio.

1288. FRANCESCO DAI LIBRI: *Madonna and Child with SS. Roch, Dominic, female Martyr and Sebastian, and donor.* Homeless.

1289. FRANCESCO DAI LIBRI:
Madonna and Child. Homeless.

1290. FRANCESCO DAI LIBRI: *Mystic Marriage
of S. Catherine, and angels.* Homeless.

1291. MICHELE DA VERONA: *Meeting of Coriolanus and Volumnia*. London, National Gallery.

1292. MICHELE DA VERONA: *Crucifixion*. Detail. Milan, Brera. *Signed and dated 1501*.

1293. MICHELE DA VERONA: *Allegorical Scene*. Fragment. Mells, Earl of Oxford and Asquith.

1294. MICHELE DA VERONA: *Crucifixion*. Detail. Milan, Brera. *Signed and dated 1501.*

1295. MICHELE DA VERONA: *Madonna and Child enthroned with SS. John Baptist, Andrew, Lawrence and Peter, and music-making Angel. Villa Estense, S. Andrea. Signed and dated 1523.*

1296. MICHELE DA VERONA: *S. Sebastian*. Piazzola, Villa Camerini.

1297. BENAGLIO: *Triptych: Madonna and Child worshipped by S. Bernardino; SS. Peter, Paul and Francis; SS. Anthony of Padua, Louis of Toulouse and Jerome. Verona, S. Bernardino. Signed. 1462.*

1299. DOMENICO MORONE: *Madonna and blessing Child.* Berlin–Dahlem, Staatliche Museen. *Signed and dated 1484.*

1298. BENAGLIO: *Madonna and Child.* Homeless.

1300. Benaglio: *S. Jerome*. Washington, National Gallery of Art, Kress Collection.
Signed.

1301–2. DOMENICO MORONE: *Organ-shutters: S. Francis, S. Bernardino*. Verona, S. Bernardino. *1481*.

1303. DOMENICO MORONE: *Presentation of the Virgin*.
Châalis, Musée Jacquemart–André.

1304. DOMENICO MORONE: *S. Blaise and the animals*. Vicenza, Pinacoteca.

1305. DOMENICO MORONE: *Madonna crowned by Angels and crowning S. Brigid, while the Christ Child gives ring to S. Catherine*. Stuttgart, Landesgalerie. *Late work.*

1306. DOMENICO MORONE: *Martyrdom of S. Blaise*. Vicenza, Pinacoteca.

1308. DOMENICO MORONE: *Detail of fresco: SS. Anthony of Padua, Bonaventura, Bernardino and Louis of Toulouse. Verona, S. Bernardino, Old Library. Dated 1503.*

1307. DOMENICO MORONE: *Detail of fresco: Madonna and Child in glory. Verona, S. Bernardino, Old Library. Dated 1503.*

1310. BONSIGNORI: *Madonna and Child enthroned with SS. Jerome and George.*
Verona, S. Bernardino. Signed and dated 1488.

1309. BONSIGNORI: *Madonna and Child enthroned with SS. Onophrius, Jerome,*
Christopher and Bishop Saint, and Altobella Avogadro. Verona, Museo di Castelvecchio.
Signed and dated 1484.

1311. BONSIGNORI: *S. Mary Magdalen*. Detail of Madonna and Child.
Verona, S. Paolo.

1312. BONSIGNORI: *Bust of Petrus Leonius*.
Homeless.

1313. BONSIGNORI: *Portrait of a man*. London,
National Gallery. *Signed and dated 1487*.

1314. BONSIGNORI: *Madonna and Child in glory and SS. Blaise, Sebastian and Juliana.*
Verona, SS. Nazaro e Celso. *1514–19.*

1315. JOSAPHAT DE ARALDIS: *S. Sebastian*. Parma, Pinacoteca.

1316. GIROLAMO DAI LIBRI: *Madonna and Child*. Homeless.
Formerly London, Lord de Saumarez. *Early work*.

1317. GIROLAMO DAI LIBRI: *Deposition*. Detail. Malcesine, Parish Church. *Early work*.

1318. GIROLAMO DAI LIBRI: *'Nativity of the Rabbits'*, *with SS. John Baptist and Jerome.*
Verona, Museo del Castelvecchio.

1319. GIROLAMO DAI LIBRI: *Miniature: Nativity.*
Cleveland, Museum of Art.

1320. GIROLAMO DAI LIBRI: *Funeral
of S. Lorenzo Giustiniani.* Detail.
Bennebrook, Frau von Pannwitz.

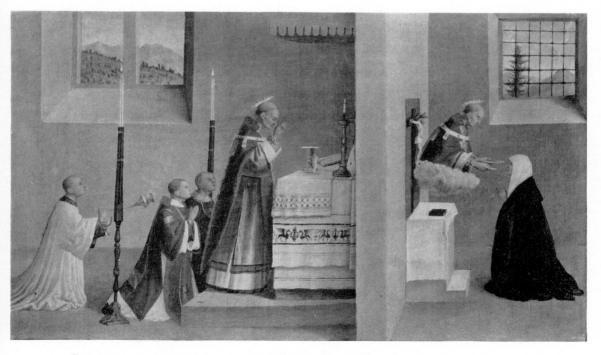

1321. GIROLAMO DAI LIBRI: *S. Lorenzo Giustiniani saying Mass and giving Communion to a woman.*
Bennebrook, Frau von Pannwitz.

1322. GIROLAMO DAI LIBRI: *Madonna and Child with SS. Anne, Joseph and Joachim, and two members of the Baughi family*. Verona, S. Paolo. *Late work.*

1323. GIROLAMO DAI LIBRI: *Madonna and Child enthroned with S. Joseph, Tobias and the Angel.*
Verona, Museo del Castelvecchio. *Signed and dated 1530.*

1324. GIROLAMO DAI LIBRI: *Christ in Galilee*. Formerly London, Mrs. Mark Hamburg.

1325. FRANCESCO MORONE: *Madonna and Child with SS. Mary Magdalen, Nicholas, John Baptist and Catherine*. Princeton, N.J., University Museum.

1326. Francesco Morone: *Christ on the Cross with the mourning Virgin and S. John Evangelist.*
Verona, S. Bernardino. *Signed and dated 1498.*

1327. FRANCESCO MORONE: *Frescoes: Busts of Olivetan worthies.* Verona, S. Maria in Organo.

1328. FRANCESCO MORONE: *Madonna and Child with SS. Martin and Augustine and Angels.*
Verona, S. Maria in Organo. *Signed and dated 1503.*

1330. Francesco Morone: *Madonna and Child*. Padua, Museo. *Signed.*

1329. Francesco Morone: *Madonna and Child*. Verona,
S. Maria Matricolare, Biblioteca. *Signed. Late work.*

1331. FRANCESCO MORONE: *Miniature: Madonna and Child with SS. Rose and Catherine.* New York, R. Lehman. *Signed.*

1332. FRANCESCO MORONE: *Madonna and Child with SS. Anthony Abbot and Onuphrius.* Berlin-East, Staatliche Museen. *Signed.*

1333. CAVAZZOLA: *Fresco: Annunciation and two Bishop Saints. Verona, SS. Nazaro e Celso. 1510–11.*

1335. CAVAZZOLA: *Madonna and Child with S. Francis.* Paris,
Musées Nationaux.

1334. CAVAZZOLA: *Madonna and Child.* Homeless.

1336. CAVAZZOLA: *Madonna and Child with young S. John Baptist and Angel.* London, National Gallery. *Signed.*

1337. CAVAZZOLA: *Madonna and Child with Infant S. John.* Verona, Museo del Castelvecchio. *Signed.*

1338. CAVAZZOLA: *Doubting Thomas, with Ascension and Descent of the Holy Ghost in the background.* Verona, Museo del Castelvecchio.

1339. CAVAZZOLA: *Panel of polyptych: Deposition*. Verona, Museo del Castelvecchio.
Signed and dated 1517.

1340. CAVAZZOLA: *Man holding laurel-branch, and his dog*. Homeless.

1341. CAVAZZOLA: *Portrait of Giulia Trivulzio.* Milan, Trivulzio Collection. *Signed and dated 1519.*

1342. CAVAZZOLA: *Bust of young woman.* Formerly Vienna, Auspitz Collection.

1343. CAVAZZOLA: *Bust of gentleman.* Prague, National Gallery.

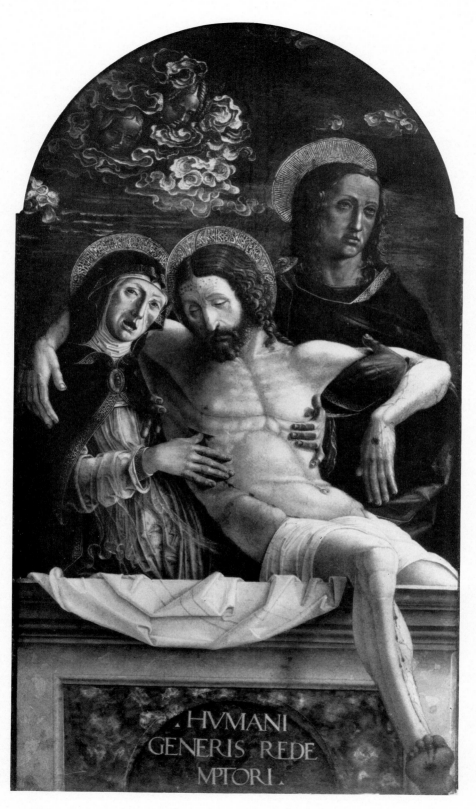

1344. BUTINONE: *Pietà*. Formerly Berlin, Kaiser-Friedrich Museum. Destroyed 1945.

1345–6. BUTINONE: *Two panels from the Life of Christ: Deposition.* Chicago, Art Institute.—*Last Judgement.* Homeless.

1347–8. BUTINONE: *Two panels from the Life of Christ: Adoration of the Magi*. London, Mrs. J. Macdonald.—*Circumcision*. Bergamo, Accademia Carrara.

1349. BUTINONE: *Fresco: Simulated circular window with Dominican Saint*. Milan, S. Maria delle Grazie. *After 1482.*

1350–51. BUTINONE: *Frescoes: Dominican Saints in niches*. Milan, S. Maria delle Grazie. *After 1482.*

1352. Butinone: *Triptych: Madonna and Child with SS. Vincent and Bernardino*. Milan, Brera. *Signed and dated 1484*.

1353. Butinone: *Predella panel: Crucifixion*. Treviglio, S. Martino. *Commissioned 1485*.

1354–5. BUTINONE: *Two details from Madonna and Child enthroned with six music-making Angels.*
Milan, Duca Gallarati Scotti.

1356. BUTINONE: *Madonna and Child enthroned with four music-making Angels, S. John Baptist and S. Justina.*
Isolabella, Palazzo Borromeo. *Signed.*

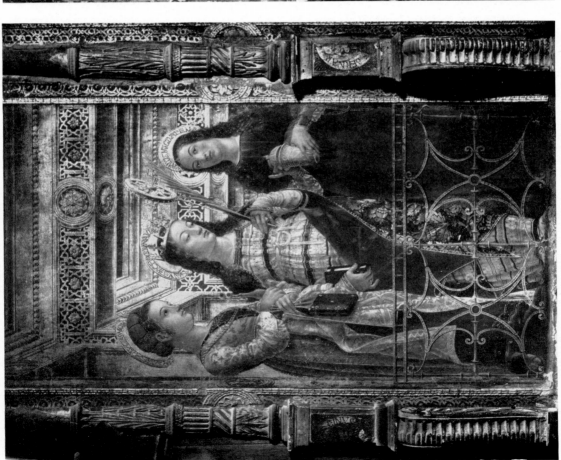

1357–58. BUTINONE AND ZENALE: *Centre and side-panels of polyptych: Three female Saints (by* ZENALE); *Madonna and Child enthroned with six Angels (Angels by* BUTINONE). Treviglio, S. Martino. *Commissioned 1485.*

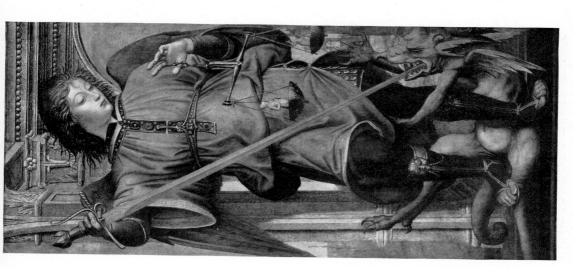

1359–61. ZENALE: *Three panels of polyptych: Madonna and All Saints. Lawrence, Kansas, University, Kress Collection.—S. Michael; S. William of Aviane and Carthusian donor. Florence, Contini Bonacossi Collection.*

1363. Zenale and Civerchio: *Madonna and Child with S. Francis.*
Homeless.

1362. Zenale: *Mocking of Christ.* Milan, Borromeo Collection.
Signed and dated 1503.

1364. ZENALE AND CIVERCHIO: *Circumcision with four Saints and Fra Jacopo Lampugnani.* Paris, Louvre. *Dated 1491.*

1365. CIVERCHIO: *Tabernacle doors: Annunciation.*
Bergamo, Accademia Carrara.

1366. ZENALE AND CIVERCHIO: *Triptych: Madonna and Child blessing donors; SS. Catherine and John Baptist;*
SS. Peter and Anthony of Padua. Milan, Ambrosiana.

1367. CIVERCHIO: *Polyptych: S. Nicholas of Tolentino in glory; S. Roch; S. Sebastian; in lunette, Pietà.*
Brescia, Pinacoteca. *Signed and dated 1495.*

1368–9. CIVERCHIO: *Pietà with SS. Sebastian, Onuphrius, Paul and Magdalen; in predella, Agony in the Garden, Incredulity of S. Thomas, Noli me tangere.* Brescia, S. Alessandro. *Signed and dated 1504.*

1370. CIVERCHIO: *Pietà*. Palermo, Chiaramonte Bordonaro Collection.

1371. CIVERCHIO: *Detail of predella: Agony in the Garden*. Brescia, S. Alessandro. *1504*.

1372. CIVERCHIO: *Madonna and Child with SS. Lawrence and John Baptist*. Lovere, Accademia Tadini.
Signed. Late work.

1373. CIVERCHIO: *Baptism of Christ*. Lovere, Accademia Tadini. *Signed and dated 1539.*

1374. BRAMANTE: *Detached fresco: Monochrome bust of man.*
Rome, Vatican, Pinacoteca.

1375. BRAMANTE: *Detached fresco: Heraclitus and Democritus.* Milan, Brera. *About 1480–5.*

1376. BRAMANTE: *Detached fresco: Man with sword.* Milan, Brera. *About 1480–5.*

1377. BRAMANTINO: *Madonna suckling the Child.*
Boston, Museum of Fine Arts.

1378. BRAMANTINO: *Madonna holding fruit and Child.*
Formerly Berlin, E. Simon.

1379. BRAMANTINO: *Jupiter visiting Philemon and Baucis.* Cologne, Wallraf-Richartz-Museum.
Early work.

1380. BRAMANTINO: *Nativity*. Milan, Ambrosiana.

1381. BRAMANTINO: *Detached frescoed lunette: Pietà.* Milan, Ambrosiana.

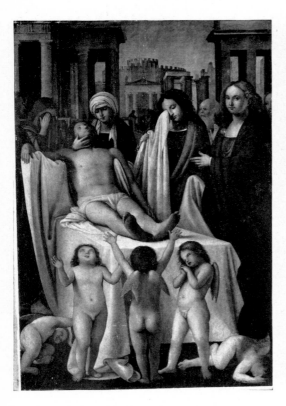

1382. BRAMANTINO: *Pietà.* Formerly Vienna, Artaria Collection.

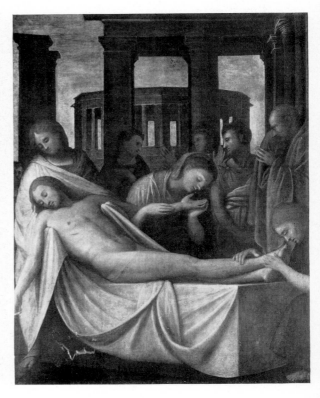

1383. BRAMANTINO: *Pietà.* Homeless.

1384. BRAMANTINO: *Crucifixion*. Milan, Brera. *Late work*.

1385. BRAMANTINO: *Tapestry: June*. Milan, Castello Sforzesco. *Soon after 1501.*

1386. Bramantino: *Tapestry: December*. Milan, Castello Sforzesco. *Soon after 1501.*

1387. MASTER OF THE SFORZA ALTARPIECE: *Fragment of altarpiece: SS. Anne and Joseph.*
Paris, Musée des Arts Décoratifs.

1388. MASTER OF THE SFORZA ALTARPIECE: *The Sforza altarpiece: Madonna and Child enthroned with the Doctors of the Church, Lodovico il Moro, Beatrice d'Este and their children.* Milan, Brera. *1494.*

1390. MASTER OF THE SFORZA ALTARPIECE: *Madonna and Child with rosary.*
Berlin-Dahlem, Staatliche Museen

1389. MASTER OF THE SFORZA ALTARPIECE: *Madonna and Child*
in niche. Berlin-Ost, Staatliche Museen

1392. MASTER OF THE SFORZA ALTARPIECE: *Madonna and Child with S. Roch presenting donor.* Florence, Cora Collection.

1391. MASTER OF THE SFORZA ALTARPIECE: *Madonna and Child with Saints and worshippers.* London, National Gallery.

1393. MASTER OF THE SFORZA ALTARPIECE: *Portrait of a Sforza prince*. Detail from plate 1388.

VERA IMAGO PRIMO GENITI LEGITIMEILE QVON ĐNI IO GZ MARIE
SFORTIE MEDIOLANI DVCIS DVM ESSET ETATIS ANOR QVINQTO

1394. Bᴇʀɴᴀʀᴅɪɴᴏ ᴅᴇ’ Cᴏɴᴛɪ: *Francesco Sforza as a boy*. Rome, Vatican. *Signed and dated 1496.*

1395. BERNARDINO DE' CONTI: *Madonna suckling the Child*. Homeless.

1396. BERNARDINO DE' CONTI: *Madonna suckling the Child* (after Leonardo's Madonna Litta). Spliska, Cerineo Castle. *Signed*.

1397. BERNARDINO DE' CONTI: *Annunciation*. Detail. Locarno, S. Maria del Sasso.

1398. BERNARDINO DE' CONTI: *Version of Leonardo's Virgin of the Rocks.*
Formerly Berlin Museen. Destroyed 1945. *Signed and dated 1522*

99. BERNARDINO DE' CONTI: *Madonna and Child with flower.*
Formerly Cambridge, Fitzwilliam Museum.

1400. BERNARDINO DE' CONTI: *Madonna and Child
in a landscape.* Milan, Ambrosiana.

1401. BERNARDINO DE' CONTI: *Charles d'Amboise*.
Saint-Amand-Montrond, Hôtel de Ville.
Signed and dated 1500.

1402. BERNARDINO DE' CONTI: *Portrait of a lady*.
Formerly Fonthill, Hugh Morrison.

1403. BERNARDINO DE' CONTI: *Portrait of middle-aged lady*. San Marino, Cal., Huntington Museum.

1404. BERNARDINO DE' CONTI: *Catellano Trivulzio*.
Brooklyn, N.Y., Museum. *Signed and dated 1505.*

1405. AMBROGIO DE PREDIS: *Music-making Angel*. Side-panel to the *Virgin of the Rocks*.
London, National Gallery.

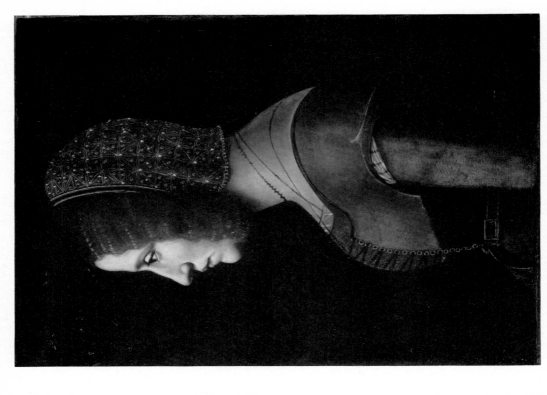

1406. AMBROGIO DE PREDIS: *Portrait of a youth.* London, National Gallery. 1407. AMBROGIO DE PREDIS: *Portrait of a lady.* London, National Gallery. *Signed and dated 1494.*

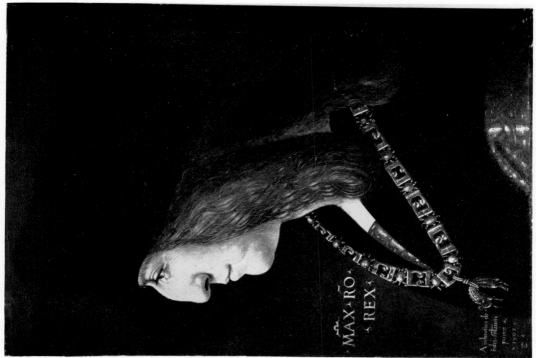

1409. AMBROGIO DE PREDIS: *Emperor Maximilian. Vienna, Kunsthistorisches Museum. Signed and dated 1502.*

1408. AMBROGIO DE PREDIS: *Francesco Sforza as a boy. Bristol, City Art Gallery.*

1410–12. MARCO D'OGGIONO: *Lower register of double triptych: Madonna and Child with music-making Angels, SS. John Baptist and Peter recommending donors. Blois, Musée.*

1413. Marco d'Oggiono: *S. Stephen.* San Simeon (Cal.), Hearst Memorial.

1414. Marco d'Oggiono: *Madonna seated in landscape with the Holy Children.* Homeless.

1415. Marco d'Oggiono: *S. Bonaventura.* San Simeon (Cal.), Hearst Memorial.

1416. MARCO D'OGGIONO: *Detached frescoed lunette: Marriage at Cana*. Milan, Brera.

1417. MARCO D'OGGIONO: *S. John Baptist worshipped by Conte Gasparo Vimercati*. Milan, S. Maria delle Grazie.

1418. Marco d'Oggiono: *The Angels Michael, Raphael and Gabriel defeat Satan.* Milan, Brera. *Signed.*

1419–20. BOLTRAFFIO: *Frescoes: Two female Saints*. Milan, S. Maurizio.

1421. BOLTRAFFIO: *Madonna and Child with book and flower*.
Formerly Berlin Museen. Destroyed 1945.

1422–3. Boltraffio: *Frescoes: Two female Saints.* Milan, S. Maurizio.

1424. Boltraffio: *Madonna and Child with book and flower.*
London, National Gallery.

1425. BOLTRAFFIO: *Skull*. (On back of plate 1426)
Chatsworth, Devonshire Collection.

1426. BOLTRAFFIO: *Bust of Costanza Bentivoglio*.
Chatsworth, Devonshire Collection.

1427. BOLTRAFFIO. *Bust of Girolamo Casio*.
Florence, Contini Bonacossi Collection.

1428. BOLTRAFFIO: *S. Sebastian*. Formerly Messina,
Eugenia Scaglione Frizzoni.

1429. BOLTRAFFIO: *Altarpiece from the Casio Chapel at Bologna: Madonna and Child with S. John Baptist, S. Sebastian, Marchione Casio and Girolamo Casio*. Paris, Louvre. *1500.*

1430. BOLTRAFFIO: *S. Barbara*. Berlin-East, Staatliche Museen. *Commissioned 1502.*

1431. ANDREA SOLARIO: *Madonna and Child*. Homeless.

1432. ANDREA SOLARIO: *Holy Family with S. Jerome*. Milan, Brera.
Signed and dated 1495.

1433. Andrea Solario: *Salome with the head of the Baptist*. New York, Metropolitan Museum. *Signed*.

1434. Andrea Solario: *Lady with prayer-book*. Budapest, Baron F. Hatvany.

1435. Andrea Solario: *Ecce homo*. Leipzig, Museum.

1436. ANDREA SOLARIO: *Salome receiving the head of S. John Baptist.* Formerly Paris, Duc d'Orléans.

1437. ANDREA SOLARIO: *Crucifixion*. Paris, Louvre. *Signed and dated 1503.*

1438. ANDREA SOLARIO: *Portrait of Cristoforo Longoni*. London, National Gallery. *Signed and dated 1505.*

1439. ANDREA SOLARIO: *Annunciation*. Paris, Musées Nationaux. *Signed and dated 1506.*

1440. ANDREA SOLARIO: *Madonna del sonno.*
Formerly Berlin, Eugen Schweizer. *About 1505.*

1441. ANDREA SOLARIO: *Bust of donor*. Fragment.
Homeless.

1442. ANDREA SOLARIO: *Rest on the Flight into Egypt*. Milan, Museo Poldi Pezzoli. *Signed and dated 1515.*

1443. GIOVANNI AGOSTINO DA LODI: *Busts of SS. Peter and John Evangelist.* Milan, Brera. *Signed. Early work.*

1444. GIOVANNI AGOSTINO DA LODI:
Madonna and Child with Angel holding bowl of fruit.
Gazzada, Cagnola Foundation.

1445. GIOVANNI AGOSTINO DA LODI: *Young man.*
Genoa, Viezzoli Collection.

1446. GIOVANNI AGOSTINO DA LODI: *Washing of Feet*. Venice, Accademia. *Dated 1500.*

1447–48. GIOVANNI AGOSTINO DA LODI: *Organ-shutter: Angel of the Annunciation; seated Evangelist.*
Berlin–Dahlem, Staatliche Museen.

1449. GIOVANNI AGOSTINO DA LODI: *Madonna and Child in landscape and busts of two donors.*
Naples, Galleria Nazionale di Capodimonte.

1450. GIOVANNI AGOSTINO DA LODI: *Madonna embracing the Child, with S. Sebastian.*
Modena, Galleria Estense.

1451–52. GIOVANNI AGOSTINO DA LODI: *Satyr playing to a nymph, with Apollo and Daphne in the background; Story of Syrinx.* Lugano, Rohoncz Collection.

1453. Giovanni Agostino da Lodi: *Adoration of the Magi*. Formerly London, William Graham.

1454–56. ALBERTINO AND MARTINO PIAZZA: *Upper register of polyptych: Assumption, S. John Baptist, S. Catherine; above, Holy Ghost, Angel and Virgin of the Annunciation. Lodi, Duomo. 1508.*

1457–59. ALBERTINO AND MARTINO PIAZZA: *Lower register of polyptych: Death of the Virgin; Bishop Saint (Bassianus?); S. Sebastian. Lodi, Palazzo del Vescovo. 1508.*

1460. ALBERTINO, SCIPIONE AND CALISTO PIAZZA: *Polyptych* (by Albertino);
side-panels with four stories of S. Anthony Abbot (by Scipione; replacing frescoes by Martino);
frescoed ornaments on pilasters and frescoed lunette round window (by Calisto and assistants).
Lodi, Incoronata, Cappella di S. Antonio Abate.

1461. ALBERTINO PIAZZA: *Adoration of the Magi*. Formerly Bergamo, Frizzoni Salis Collection.
1462. ALBERTINO PIAZZA: *Madonna and Child enthroned*. Lodi, Museo Civico.

1463. ALBERTINO PIAZZA: *Triptych: S. Nicholas enthroned, S. John Baptist and Bishop Saint,
S. Clare and Tobias with the Angel*. Formerly New York, Hearst Collection.

1464. MARTINO PIAZZA: *Detached fresco from Incoronata: S. Anthony Abbot disputing*. Lodi, Museo Civico.

1466. MARTINO PIAZZA: *Madonna and Child with S. Elizabeth and Infant S. John*. Rome, Museo di Palazzo Venezia.

1465. MARTINO PIAZZA: *S. John Baptist in the wilderness*. London, National Gallery.

1468. ALBERTINO AND MARTINO PIAZZA: *Adoration of the Shepherds.*
Milan, Sessa Fumagalli Collection. *Dated 1520.*

1467. ALBERTINO AND MARTINO PIAZZA: *Coronation of the Virgin.*
Lodi, Incoronata. *1519.*

1469. BERGOGNONE: *Madonna and Child enthroned with Angels and SS. Jerome, Gregory, Ambrose, Augustine recommending donor, Felinus, Gratinianus, Carpoforus and Fidelis.* Arona, SS. Gratiniano e Felino. *Early work.*

1470. BERGOGNONE: *Crucifixion*. Pavia, Certosa, Church. *Signed and dated 1490.*

1471. BERGOGNONE: *Frescoes: Apostle in roundel and simulated window with Carthusian monks.*
Pavia, Certosa, Church, Transept.

1472. BERGOGNONE: *Circumcision*. Lodi, Incoronata.

1474. BERGOGNONE: *Christ on the way to Golgotha and Carthusian monks.*
Pavia, Museo Malaspina. *Before 1497.*

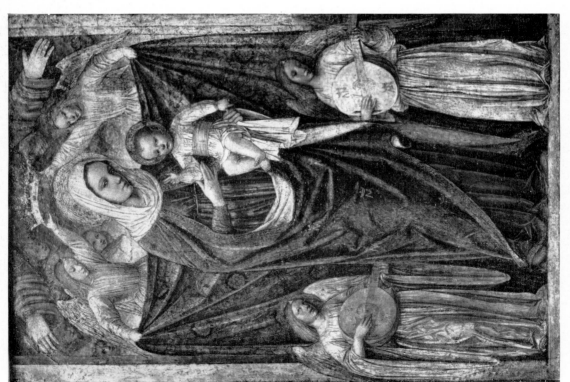

1473. BERGOGNONE: *Detached fresco: Madonna and Child with Angels.*
Milan, Brera. *1495.*

1476. BERGOGNONE: *Nativity with two Angels.*
Formerly Milan, Crespi Collection.

1475. BERGOGNONE: *Baptism of Christ.* Melegnano, Parish Church.
Signed and dated 1506.

1477. BERGOGNONE: *Madonna and Child on clouds*. Homeless.

1478. BERGOGNONE: *Madonna and blessing Child with rosary*. Rome, Visconti Venosta Collection.

1479. BERGOGNONE. *Madonna suckling the Child*. Formerly Arcore, Vittadini Collection.

1480. BERGOGNONE: *Madonna in glory with the Holy Children and S. Roch below.*
Milan, Brera. *Signed.*

1481. LUINI: *Frescoed lunette: Mocking of Christ*. Milan, S. Giorgio al Palazzo. *1516*.

1482. LUINI: *Fresco: Mourning over the Dead Christ*. Milan, S. Giorgio al Palazzo. *1516*.

1483. LUINI: *Detached fresco from S. Maria della Pace: S. Joseph's Dream.* Milan, Brera. *1518–20.*

1484. LUINI: *Detached fresco from Casa Rabia: Naiads and Tritons.* Detail. Berlin-East, Staatliche Museen.

1485. LUINI: *Detached fresco from Villa Pelucca: Bathing girls*. Milan, Brera. *1520–3*.

1486. LUINI: *Detached fresco from Casa Rabia: Europa seated on the bull*. Detail. Berlin-East, Staatliche Museen.

1487. LUINI: *Detached fresco from Casa Rabia: Procris and the unicorn.*
Washington, National Gallery of Art, Kress Collection.

1488. LUINI: *Detached fresco from Villa Pelucca: Angels carrying S. Catherine to Mount Sinai.*
Milan, Brera. *1520–23.*

1489. LUINI: *Detached fresco from Villa Pelucca: Gathering of the manna.*
Milan, Brera. *1520–23.*

1490. LUINI: *Madonna and Child with Infant S. John in landscape.*
Paris, Baronne Edouard de Rothschild.

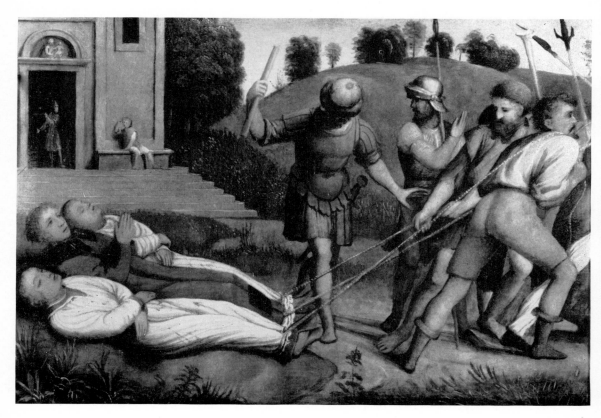

1491. LUINI: *Predella panel from Torriani polyptych: SS. Sisinius, Martyrius and Alexander dragged by their feet.*
Los Angeles, Museum of Art, Norton Simon Foundation.

1492. LUINI: *Centre panel from Torriani polyptych: Madonna and Child enthroned with SS. Sisinius and Martyrius*. Turin, Di Rovasenda Collection. *1524 or after.*

1493. LUINI: *Frescoed wall dividing the nuns from the faithful: S. Sigismund of Burgundy offers the church to S. Mauritius.* Milan, S. Maurizio. *1522–24.*

1494. LUINI: *Fresco: Circumcision*. Saronno, S. Maria dei Miracoli. *1525*.

1496. CESARE MAGNI: *Holy Family with Infant S. John*. Milan, Brera.

1495. CESARE MAGNI: *Circumcision*. Bonn, Landesmuseum.

1498. CESARE MAGNI: *Madonna and Child blessing Infant S. John in landscape.* Bergamo, Accademia Carrara.

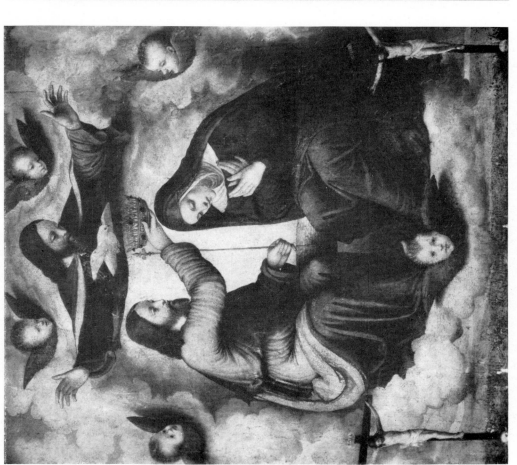

1497. CESARE MAGNI: *Coronation of the Virgin.* Milan, Donna Sessa Fumagalli.

1499. CESARE MAGNI: *Adoration of the Magi*. Isolabella, Palazzo Borromeo.

1501. CESARE MAGNI: *Madonna and Child with SS. Peter and Jerome.* Milan, Ambrosiana. *Signed and dated 1530.*

1500. CESARE MAGNI: *Madonna and Child with SS. Sebastian and Roch.* Formerly Berlin-East, Staatliche Museen.

1503. Cesare da Sesto: *Holy Family with S. Catherine*. Rome, Miss Anderson.

1502. Cesare da Sesto (?): *Madonna and Child with S. Elizabeth, Infant S. John and S. Michael holding scales*. Paris, Louvre.

1505. CESARE DA SESTO: *S. John Baptist in the wilderness.*
Balcarres, Earl of Crawford and Balcarres.

1504. CESARE DA SESTO (?): *S. John Baptist in the wilderness.*
Glasgow, City Art Gallery.

1506. Cesare da Sesto: *Panels from polyptych: S. Roch, S. Christopher, S. Sebastian, Madonna and Child, S. John Baptist, S. John Evangelist.* Milan, Castello Sforzesco.

1507. CESARE DA SESTO: *Adoration of the Magi*. Naples, Galleria Nazionale di Capodimonte.

1509. ANDREA DA SALERNO: *Nativity.*

1508. CESARE DA SESTO. *Madonna and Child enthroned with SS. George and John Baptist.*

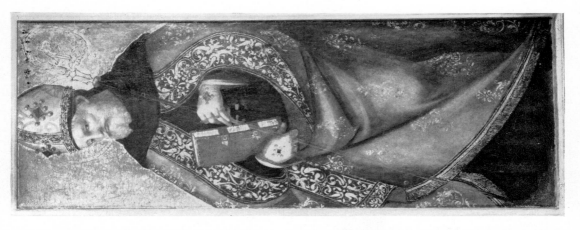

1510–12. ANDREA DA SALERNO: *Panels from polyptych: Madonna of Mercy, S. Anthony Abbot with donor, S. Augustine. Salerno, Museo Provinciale. 1512.*

1513. Andrea da Salerno: *Polyptych: Madonna and Child, S. John Baptist, S. Catherine; above, Crucifixion, S. Benedict, S. Scholastica.* Naples, SS. Severino e Sosio.

1515. ANDREA DA SALERNO: S. Benedict gives Maurus and Placidus the Benedictine rule. Montecassino, Abbazia.

1514. ANDREA DA SALERNO: S. Nicholas enthroned, with the three girls without dowry on his right and the three youths raised to life on his left. Naples, Galleria Nazionale di Capodimonte. 1517–18.

1516. Francesco Napolitano: *Madonna and Child.*
Zürich, Kunsthaus. *Signed.*

1517. Francesco Napolitano: *Madonna and Child.*
Milan, Brera.

1519. FRANCESCO NAPOLITANO: *Madonna and Child enthroned with
SS. John Baptist and Sebastian. Detail. Zürich, Kunsthaus. Signed.*

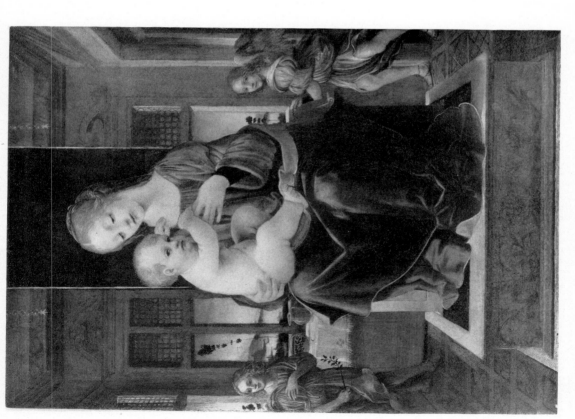

1518. FRANCESCO NAPOLITANO: *Madonna and Child enthroned with two Angels.
Stockholm, National Museum.*

1520. GIAMPIETRINO: *Madonna and Child with SS. Michael and Jerome*. Budapest, Museum of Fine Arts.

1521. GIAMPIETRINO: *Madonna of the cherries*.
Budapest, Museum of Fine Arts.

1522. GIAMPIETRINO: *Madonna and Child*. Formerly
London, Mr. Hallam Murray.

1523. Giampietrino: *Egeria*. Milan, Vonwiller Collection.

1524. GIAMPIETRINO: *Madonna and Child with SS. John Baptist and Jerome*. Pavia, S. Marino.

1525. GIAMPIETRINO: *Nativity*. Lugano, Museo di Belle Arti.

1527. GIAMPIETRINO: *Madonna and Child with Infant S. John.*
Formerly New York, R. M. Hurd.

1526. GIAMPIETRINO: *Madonna suckling the Child.*
Milan, Crespi Collection.

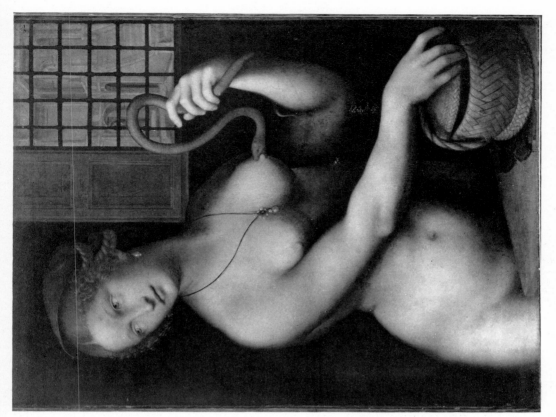

1529. GIAMPIETRINO: *Cleopatra*. Paris, Louvre.

1528. GIAMPIETRINO: *Abundance with cornucopia.*
Isolabella, Palazzo Borromeo.

1530. SODOMA: *Tondo: Holy Family with Infant S. John and two Angels.*
Formerly London, Captain Holford.

1531. SODOMA: *Detail of fresco: S. Benedict appears in a dream to sleeping monks with a model of the monastery,
and builders at work.* Monteoliveto, Abbazia. *1505–08.*

1532. SODOMA: *Detail of fresco: S. Benedict obtains flour for his monks.*
Monteoliveto, Abbazia. *1505–08.*

1533. SODOMA: *Fresco: SS. Maurus and Placidus entrusted to S. Benedict. Monteoliveto, Abbazia. 1505–08.*

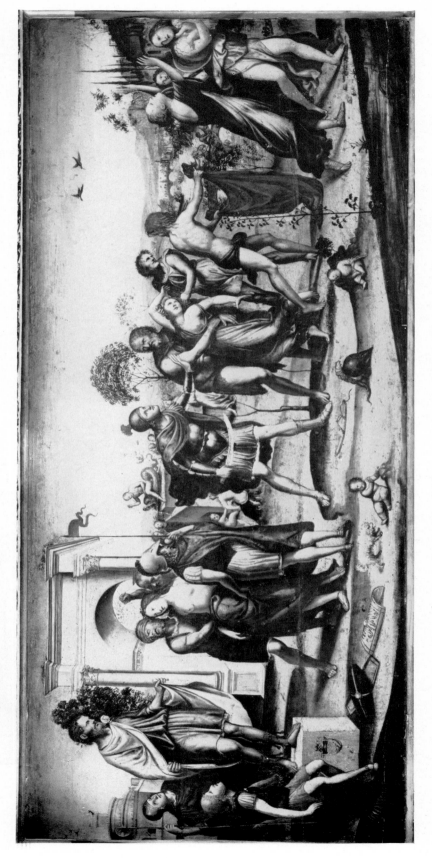

1534. SODOMA: *Front of cassone: Rape of the Sabine women*. Rome, Galleria Nazionale, Palazzo Barberini. *About 1508*.

1535. SODOMA: *Holy Family.*
Munich, Alte Pinakothek.

1536. SODOMA: *Holy Family with Infant S. John.*
Siena, Società Esecutori Pie Disposizioni.

1537. SODOMA: *Predella panel: Flagellation.* Budapest, Museum of Fine Arts.

1538. SODOMA: *Lucretia*. Paris, Duc de Trévise.

1539. SODOMA: *Detail of fresco of Last Supper: Judas.* Florence, Monteoliveto.

1540. SODOMA: *Fresco: S. Catherine praying at the execution of a Sienese youth*. Detail.
Siena, S. Domenico. *1526*.

1541. SODOMA: *Frescoes: Scenes from the Life of S. Catherine. Siena, S. Domenico. 1526.*

1542–3. SODOMA: *Frescoes: S. Victor, S. Ansanus.* Siena, Palazzo Pubblico, Sala del Mappamondo. *1529.*

1544. SODOMA: *Adoration of the Magi*. Siena, S. Agostino. *Before 1533*.

1545. SODOMA: *Resurrection*. Naples, Galleria Nazionale di Capodimonte. *Dated 1534*.

1546. TAMAGNI: *Fresco: Madonna and Child enthroned, crowned by two Angels, flanked by S. Jerome and S. Gregory.* Montalcino, Vecchio Spedale. *1510–12.*

1547. TAMAGNI: *Monochrome frescoes: Judith, Lucretia, Scipio and Plato.* Montalcino, Vecchio Spedale. *1510–12.*

1548. TAMAGNI: *Detail of fresco of Birth of the Virgin.*
Montalcino, S. Francesco. *1511.*

1549. TAMAGNI: *Portrait of a lady.* Homeless.

1550. TAMAGNI: *Birth of the Virgin and female donor.* Detail. San Gimignano, S. Agostino.
Signed and dated 1523.

1551. TAMAGNI: *Madonna and Child enthroned with SS. John Baptist, John Gualbert, Benedict and Jerome, and two putti.* San Gimignano, S. Girolamo. *Signed and dated 1522.*

1552. TAMAGNI: *Madonna della Cintola with SS. Sebastian and Roch.* Montalcino,
Madonna del Soccorso. *Signed and dated 1527.*

1553. Tamagni (on Pacchia's design): *Fresco: S. Catherine of Siena heals Matteo Cenni from the plague. Siena, Santuario Cateriniano, S. Caterina in Fontebranda.*

1554. PACCHIA: *Fresco: S. Catherine of Siena rescues Fra Tommaso della Forte and his companions attacked by robbers. Detail* Siena, Santuario Cateriniano, S. Caterina in Fontebranda.

1555–6. PACCHIA: *Bierheads: S. Bernardino of Siena with two Angels; Madonna and Child with four Angels.* Munich, Alte Pinakothek.

1557. PACCHIA: *Fresco: Birth of the Virgin.* Siena, S. Bernardino. *1518.*

1558. PACCHIA: *Annunciation and Visitation*. Siena, Pinacoteca. *1518.*

1559. PACCHIA: *Holy Family with Infant S. John.*
Formerly London, Duke of Westminster.

1560. PACCHIA: *Annunciation.* Siena, Heirs of E. Martini.

1561. PACCHIA: *Fresco: S. Agnes of Montepulciano lying in state*. Detail. Siena, Santuario Cateriniano,
S. Caterina in Fontebranda.

1562. Pacchia: *Tondo: Madonna and Child with Infant S. John.* Florence, Uffizi.

1563. PACCHIA: *Tondo: Madonna and Child with Infant S. John.*
Formerly London, Fairfax Murray.

1564. PACCHIA: *Rape of the Sabine women.* Sutton Place, J. Paul Getty Collection.

1565. PACCHIA: *Coronation of the Virgin with SS. John Baptist, Peter and Paul.* Siena, S. Spirito.

1566. BRESCIANINO: *Madonna and Child with SS. Catherine,
Joseph(?) and Infant John.* Homeless.

1567. BRESCIANINO: *Predella panel: Resurrection.* Dublin, Judge James A. Murnaghan.

1568. BRESCIANINO: *Madonna and Child with Infant S. John.*
Formerly Stockholm, R. Petre Collection.

1569. BRESCIANINO: *Portable altarpiece: Mourning Virgin, S. John Evangelist and S. Mary Magdalen round a bronze Crucifix; S. Augustine; S. Jerome.* Siena, Palazzo Chigi Saracini.

1570. BRESCIANINO: *Lady in turban and fur.*
Rome, Galleria Nazionale, Palazzo Barberini.

1571. BRESCIANINO: *Bust of young woman.* Formerly
Berlin, Schweitzer Collection.

1572. BRESCIANINO: *S. Mary Magdalen.* Homeless.

1573. BRESCIANINO: *Madonna and Child.* Formerly
Siena, Ugurgeri Collection.

1574. BRESCIANINO: *Venus and Cupids in niche*. Rome, Galleria Borghese.

1575. BECCAFUMI: *S. Paul enthroned, with his Conversion and Martyrdom in the background.*
Siena, S. Maria Assunta, Museo del Duomo.

1576. BECCAFUMI: *Tanaquil; Marcia*. London, National Gallery.

1577. BECCAFUMI: *Feast of Lupercalia*. Florence, Contesse Martelli.

1578. BECCAFUMI: *Tondo: Holy Family with Infant S. John.*
Formerly Rome, Cav. Lattanzio Marri Mignanelli.

1579. BECCAFUMI: *Martyrdom of S. Lucy.* Formerly Berlin, Museum. Destroyed 1945.

1580. BECCAFUMI: *Nativity*. Siena, S. Martino. *About 1523.*

1581. BECCAFUMI: *Frescoed ceiling: Scenes from Roman history.* Siena, Palazzo Bindi Sergardi.

1582. BECCAFUMI: *Frescoed ceiling: Scenes from Roman history*. Siena, Palazzo Bindi Sergardi.

1583. Beccafumi: *Altarpiece from S. Spirito: Mystic Marriage of S. Catherine with SS. Peter, Sigismund, Francis, Bernardino, Catherine of Alexandria and Paul*. Siena, Palazzo Chigi Saracini. *Before 1528*.

1584. BECCAFUMI: *Book-cover: The Magistrati del Concistoro offer the keys of Siena to the Madonna delle Grazie during the siege of 1526.* Chatsworth, Devonshire Collection.

1585. BECCAFUMI: *Predella panel to the S. Spirito altarpiece: S. Bernardino preaching.* Formerly London, A. Scharf.

1586. BECCAFUMI: *S. Catherine receiving stigmata*. Homeless.

1587. BECCAFUMI: *Flight of Clelia*. Belgrade, White Palace.

1588. BECCAFUMI: *S. Michael defeats Satan*. Siena, S. Maria del Carmine. *Before 1535*.

1589. BECCAFUMI: *Moses breaks the Tables of the Law*. Pisa, Duomo. 1537–9.

1590. BECCAFUMI: *Head of bronze Angel*. Siena, S. Maria Assunta (Duomo). *1548–50*.

1591. BECCAFUMI: *Marble intarsia on his design: The Golden Calf*. Siena, S. Maria Assunta (Duomo). *1531*.

THE RENAISSANCE IN BOLOGNA, CREMONA, LODI AND BRESCIA

1591-a. FRANCIA: *View of Bologna*. Detail from the *Madonna del Terremoto*.
Bologna, Palazzo Comunale. *Dated 1505.*

1592. FRANCIA: *Holy Family*. Berlin-Dahlem, Staatliche Museen. *Signed*.

1593. FRANCIA: *Portrait of Bernardino Vanni*. Formerly Paris, Heugel Collection.

1594. FRANCIA: *Predella panel: Nativity*. Glasgow Art Gallery.

1595. FRANCIA: *S. John Baptist*. Turin, Accademia Albertina.

1596. FRANCIA: *Madonna and Child*. New Haven (Conn.), Yale University Art Gallery. *Signed and dated 1495.*

1597. FRANCIA: *Predella panel: Baptism of Christ*. Lisbon, Gulbenkian Foundation.

1598. FRANCIA: *Madonna and Child with SS. John Baptist, Monica, Augustine, Francis, Procolo and Sebastian, a music-making Angel and Bartolomeo Felicini as donor.* Bologna, Pinacoteca. *Signed and dated 1494.*

1599. FRANCIA: *Centre panel of altarpiece: Adoration of the Child with S. Augustine and Anton Galeazzo Bentivoglio as donor.* Bologna, Pinacoteca. *Dated 1499.*

1601. FRANCIA: *Madonna of the cherries*. Formerly Taymouth Castle, Marquess of Breadalbane.

1600. FRANCIA: *S. Francis*. Florence, Contini Bonacossi Collection.

1603. FRANCIA: *Annunciation and SS. John Evangelist, Francis, Bernardino and George.* Bologna, Pinacoteca. *Signed and dated 1500.*

1602. FRANCIA. *S. Roch.* New York, Metropolitan Museum. *Dated 1502.*

1604. COSTA: *Fresco: S. Urban converts Valerian.* Bologna, S. Giacomo Maggiore. *1504–6.*

1605. FRANCIA: *Fresco: Marriage of S. Cecilia and Valerian.* Bologna, S. Giacomo Maggiore. *1506.*

1606. WORKSHOP OF COSTA: *Fresco: Baptism of S. Valerian*. Bologna, S. Giacomo Maggiore. *1506*.

1607. FRANCIA: *Fresco: Burial of S. Cecilia*. Bologna, S. Giacomo Maggiore. *1506*.

1608. FRANCIA: *Lunette: Pietà with female Saint.* Berlin–Ost, Staatliche Museen.

1609. FRANCIA: *Madonna and Child standing on parapet.* Leipzig, Museum. *Signed and dated 1517.*

1610. FRANCIA: *Madonna and Child.* Wallington, Northumberland, Sir George Trevelyan.

1611. FRANCIA: *Adoration of the Magi*. Detail. Dresden, Gallery.

1612. FRANCIA: *Madonna and Child with S. Francis.*
Formerly New York, Stanley Mortimer. *Late work.*

1613. FRANCIA: *Lucretia*. Dublin,
National Gallery of Ireland.

1614. FRANCIA: *Angels and landscape round a Madonna by Sano di Pietro.*
Bologna, SS. Vitale e Agricola. *Late work.*

1615. FERRARESE-BOLOGNESE, 1450–1525: *Assumption of S. Mary of Egypt*. Ferrara, Pinacoteca.

1615a. FERRARESE-BOLOGNESE, 1450–1525: *S. Francis receiving stigmata*. Homeless.

1616. FERRARESE-BOLOGNESE, 1450–1525 (same hand as plate 1615): *Christ on the Cross with mourning Virgin and S. John Evangelist*. New Haven (Conn.), Yale University Art Gallery.

1618. Maineri (after Solario): *Christ carrying the Cross.*
Modena, Galleria Estense.

1617. Maineri (after Solario): *Head of the Baptist on a platter.*
Milan, Brera. *Signed.*

1619. MAINERI: *Holy Family, with statues of Adam and Eve in the background. Milan, Treccani Collection.*

1620. MAINERI: *Madonna and Child. Turin, Accademia Albertina. Signed.*

1621. MAINERI: *Madonna and Child enthroned between S. Cosmas and S. Damian, with SS. Eustace and George in the background.* Formerly Allington Castle, Lord Conway.

1622. MAINERI: *Flagellation with kneeling Dominican*. Milan, Dr. Grieco.

1623. Ferrarese-Bolognese 1450–1525 (Maineri and Costa?): *Lunette to the Strozzi altarpiece: Pietà*. Ferrara, Massari Zavaglia Collection. *1494–1500*.

1624. Maineri: *Adoration of the Shepherds*. Homeless.

1625. FERRARESE-BOLOGNESE 1450–1525 (MAINERI AND COSTA?): *The Strozzi altarpiece: Madonna and Child enthroned with SS. William and John Baptist.* London, National Gallery. *1494–1500.*

1626. COSTA: *Madonna and Child enthroned with Giovanni II Bentivoglio, his wife, four sons and seven daughters*. Bologna, S. Giacomo Maggiore. *Signed and dated 1488*.

1627. Costa: *Madonna and Child enthroned with SS. James, Jerome, Sebastian and George.*
Bologna, S. Petronio. *Signed and dated 1492.*

1628. COSTA: *Fresco: Triumph of Fame*. Bologna, S. Giacomo Maggiore. *1490*.

1629. COSTA: *Fresco: Triumph of Death*. Bologna, S. Giacomo Maggiore. *1490*.

1630. COSTA: *Madonna and Child enthroned with SS. Augustine, Posidonius, John and Francis.*
Bologna, S. Giovanni in Monte. *Signed and dated 1497.*

1631. COSTA: *Cardinal Bibbiena and penitent S. Jerome in background.*
Formerly Downton Castle, Major Kincaid Lennox.

1632. COSTA: *Predella panel to Francia's Nativity* (plate 1599): *Adoration of the Magi.* Milan, Brera.
Signed and dated 1499.

1633. COSTA: *Venus*. Bologna, Conte Giuseppe Scarselli.

1634. COSTA: *Circumcision*. Formerly Berlin, Museum; destroyed 1945. *Signed and dated 1502.*

1635. COSTA: *Kingdom of Comus*. Paris, Louvre. 1511–12.

1636. COSTA: *The Commander Federico Gonzaga and his entourage. Detail.* Prague, National Gallery. *1522.*

1637. ALENI: *Madonna and Child enthroned with S. Anthony of Padua and S. Francis recommending a monk.* Cremona, Pinacoteca. *Signed and dated 1500.*

1638. ALENI: *Madonna adoring the Christ Child with SS. John Baptist and Anthony Abbot and music-making Angel.* Cremona, Pinacoteca. *Signed and dated 1515.*

1639. ALENI (?): *Madonna adoring the Child, and a Saint*. Lille, Musée.

1640. ALENI: *Madonna and Child*. Formerly London, Benson Collection. *Signed*.

1641. ALENI: *Fresco: Last Supper*. Detail. Cremona, S. Sigismondo. *1508*.

1642–3. ALENI: *Organ-shutters: Angel and Virgin of Annunciation*. Cremona, Duomo.

1644. ALENI: *Detail of fresco: S. Jerome surrounded by monks*. Cremona, S. Sigismondo.

1645. GALEAZZO CAMPI: *Madonna and Child.*
Cambridge, Fitzwilliam Museum. *Signed.*

1646. GALEAZZO CAMPI: *Madonna and Child with SS. Blaise and Anthony Abbot.* Detail. Milan, Brera.
Signed and dated 1517.

1647. GALEAZZO CAMPI: *Centre panel of polyptych: Nativity.* Cremona, S. Maria Maddalena.

1648. GALEAZZO CAMPI: *Assumption*. Cremona, S. Abbondio.

1649–50. BOCCACCINO: *Madonna and Child*. Homeless. *Female Saint*. Formerly London, Lord Rennell of Rodd.

1651. BOCCACCINO: *Death of the Virgin*. Detail. Ferrara, Pinacoteca.

1652. BOCCACCINO: *S. Jerome in the wilderness.* Cremona, Pinacoteca. *Signed.*

1653. BOCCACCINO: *Fresco: Christ in glory and Saints*. Detail. Cremona, Duomo.
Signed and dated 1506.

1654. BOCCACCINO: *Fresco: Annunciation*. Detail. Cremona, Duomo.

1655. BOCCACCINO: *Fresco: Joachim and the Angel*. Cremona, Duomo. *Signed and dated 1515.*

1656. BOCCACCINO: *Fresco: Marriage of the Virgin*. Detail. Cremona, Duomo. *Signed and dated 1515.*

1657. BOCCACCINO: *Fresco: Birth of the Virgin*. Detail. Cremona, Duomo. *Signed and dated 1514.*

1658. BOCCACCINO: *Fresco: Meeting at the Golden Gate*. Detail. Cremona, Duomo.
Signed and dated 1515.

1660. Boccaccino: *Madonna and Child enthroned. Detail.* Formerly Vienna, Liechtenstein Collection.

1659. Boccaccino: *Madonna and Child.* Boston, Museum of Fine Arts.

1661. BOCCACCINO: *Sacra Conversazione (or Mystic Marriage of S. Catherine with SS. Peter, Lucy and John Baptist).* Venice, Accademia. *Signed.*

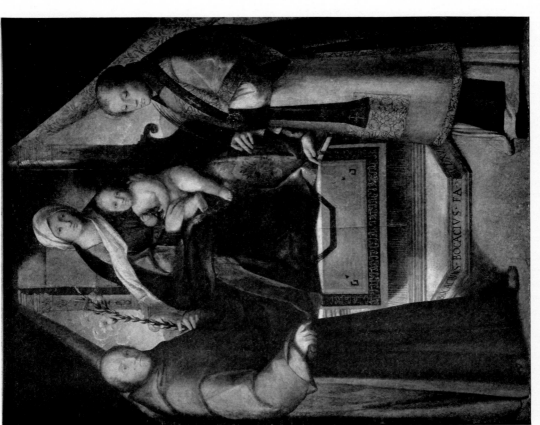

1662. BOCCACCINO: *Madonna and Child enthroned with SS. Anthony of Padua and Vincent.* Cremona, Pinacoteca. Signed and dated 1518.

1663. BOCCACCINO: *Nativity with S. Jerome.* Budapest, Museum of Fine Arts.

1664. BOCCACCINO: *Fresco: Christ disputing with the Doctors. Cremona, Duomo. Signed and dated 1518.*

1665. ALTOBELLO MELONE: *Centre panel of polyptych: Madonna and Child enthroned.*
Sands Point, L.I., Mrs. Hannah D. Rabinowitz.

1666–8. ALTOBELLO MELONE: *Panels from Picenardi Triptych: Tobias and the Angel; S. Helena.* Oxford. Ashmolean Museum.—*Madonna and Child.* Columbia (Mo.), University of Missouri, Kress Study Collection.

1669. ALTOBELLO MELONE: *Predella panel from Picenardi Triptych: Finding of the True Cross.* Algiers, Musée.

1671. ALTOBELLO MELONE: *Venus and Cupid*. Formerly Stockholm,
D. L. Telander.

1670. ALTOBELLO MELONE: *Portrait of a lady*. Rome, Opere recuperate.

1672. ALTOBELLO MELONE: *Fresco: Massacre of the Innocents. Detail.* Cremona, Duomo. *1516/7.*

1673. ALTOBELLO MELONE: *Fresco: Flight into Egypt. Detail. Cremona, Duomo. 1516/7.*

1674. Altobello Melone: *Frescoes: Betrayal of Christ and Christ before Caiaphas. Cremona, Duomo. Signed. 1517/8.*

1675. CALISTO PIAZZA: *Concert*. Philadelphia, John G. Johnson Collection.

1676. CALISTO PIAZZA: *Open-air Concert*. Formerly Vienna, Bertha Morelli.

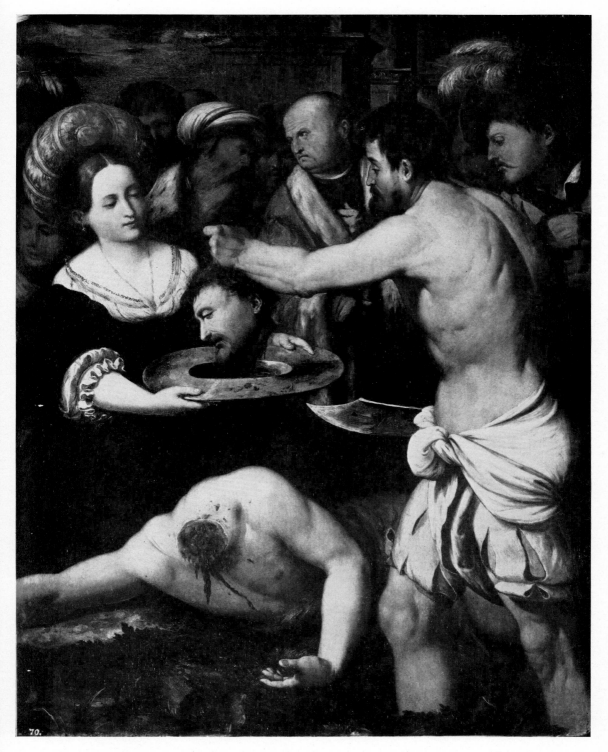

1677. CALISTO PIAZZA: *Beheading of S. John Baptist*. Venice, Accademia. *Signed and dated 1526.*

1678. CALISTO PIAZZA: *Visitation*. Brescia, S. Maria in Calchera. *Signed and dated 1525.*

1679. CALISTO PIAZZA: *S. John Baptist preaching*. Lodi, Incoronata, Cappella del Battista.

1681. CALISTO PIAZZA: *Beheading of S. John Baptist.* Lodi, Incoronata, Cappella del Battista. *Signed and dated 1530.*

1680. CALISTO PIAZZA: *Madonna and Child with SS. John Baptist and Jerome.* Milan, Brera. *Signed.*

1682. CALISTO PIAZZA: *Lower register of polytych: Two Warrior Saints, Massacre of the Innocents, Saintly Pope and Bishop. Lodi, Duomo. 1529–32.*

1683. CALISTO PIAZZA: *Fresco: Assumption*. Detail. Erbanno, S. Maria di Restello.

1684. CALISTO PIAZZA: *Fresco: S. George killing the dragon*. Detail. Erbanno, S. Maria di Restello.

1685. ROMANINO: *Mourning over the dead Christ*. Detail. Venice, Accademia. *Signed and dated 1510.*

1686. ROMANINO: *Madonna and Child with SS. Louis of Toulouse, Roch and three Angels.*
Formerly Berlin, Museum. Destroyed 1945.

1687. ROMANINO: *Supper in the House of Simon*. Detail. Brescia, S. Giovanni Evangelista. *1521–4*.

1688. ROMANINO: *Madonna and Child*. Homeless.

1689. ROMANINO: *Detail of polyptych: S. Alexander.*
London, National Gallery. *Dated 1525*.

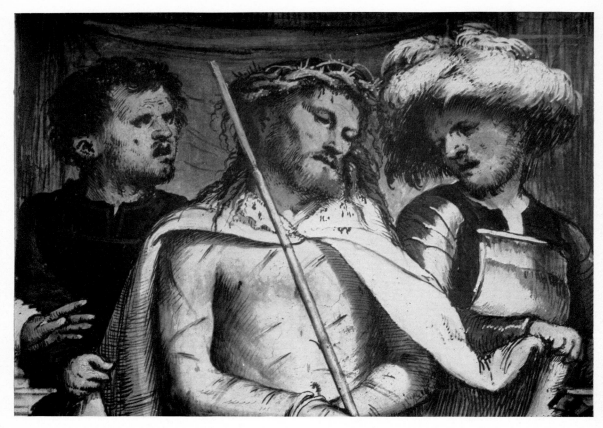

1690. ROMANINO: *Fresco: Ecce homo*. Detail. Cremona, Duomo. *1519*.

1691. ROMANINO: *Organ-shutter: Sacrifice of Isaac*. Detail. Asola, Duomo.

1692. ROMANINO: *S. Anthony of Padua worshipped by Conte Cicala.* Salò, Duomo. *Signed and dated 1529.*

1693. ROMANINO: *Frescoed loggia*. Trento, Castello del Buonconsiglio. *1531–2*.

1694. ROMANINO: *Frescoed hall*. Trento, Castello del Buonconsiglio. *1531–2*.

1695. Romanino: *Frescoes on staircase*. Trento, Castello del Buonconsiglio. *1531–2*.

1696. ROMANINO: *Detail of fresco: Martino Malpaga and two workmen.*
Trento, Castello del Buonconsiglio. *1531–2.*

1697. ROMANINO: *Fresco: Marriage of the Virgin.* Detail. Bienno, S. Maria Annunziata.

1698. ROMANINO: *Fresco: Descent into Limbo*. Pisogne, S. Maria della Neve. *Before 1534*.

1699. MORETTO: *Christ holding the Cross, worshipped by donor.* Bergamo, Accademia Carrara.
Formerly dated 1518.

1700. MORETTO: *Last Supper, and Prophets*. Brescia, S. Giovanni Evangelista, Cappella del Sacramento.
1521–4.

1701–2. MORETTO: *Two details from Christ in Emmaus*. Brescia, Pinacoteca.

1704. MORETTO: *Coronation of the Virgin.*
Vienna, Baron K. Lamprecht.

1703. MORETTO: *Coronation of the Virgin.* Detail.
Brescia, SS. Nazzaro e Celso. 1534.

1705. MORETTO: *Massacre of the Innocents. Brescia, S. Giovanni Evangelista. 1530–2.*

1706. MORETTO: *The Virgin and S. Elizabeth with the Holy Children appearing to two Camaldolese friars.*
Formerly Berlin, Museum. Destroyed 1945. *Signed and dated 1541.*

1707. MORETTO: *Portrait of a lady*. Milan, Sola Collection.

1708. MORETTO: *Holy Family with Infant S. John*. Rome, Visconti Venosta Collection.

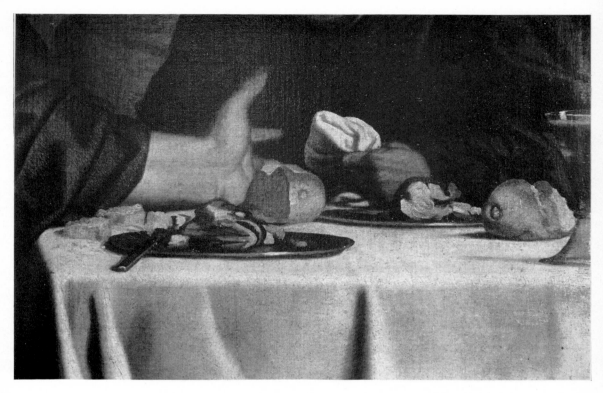

1709. MORETTO: *Detail from Christ in the House of Simon.* Brescia, S. Maria in Calchera.

1710. MORETTO: *Detail from Nativity with Saints.* Brescia, Pinacoteca.

1711. MORETTO: *Ecce Homo and Angel*. Brescia, Pinacoteca.

1712. ASPERTINI: *Amazonomachia*. Homeless.

1713. ASPERTINI: *Adoration of the Shepherds*. Berlin-Ost, Staatliche Museen. *Signed.*

1714. ASPERTINI: *Nativity with SS. George, Francis, John Baptist, Jerome, Eustace and Sebastian, and two donors.*
Bologna, Pinacoteca. *Signed. About 1504.*

1715. ASPERTINI: *Predella panel: Adoration of the Shepherds, Adoration of the Magi.* Homeless. *Early work.*

1716–17. ASPERTINI: *Predella panel*: *Meeting at the Golden Gate, Birth of the Virgin, Presentation of the Virgin, Marriage of the Virgin*. Florence, Casa Strozzi.

1719. ASPERTINI: *Detail of fresco: Funeral of Valerian and Tiburtius.*
Bologna, S. Giacomo Maggiore. *1506.*

1718. ASPERTINI: *Miniature: Nativity.* London, British Museum,
Albani Book of Hours. *Signed.*

1720. ASPERTINI: *Fresco in soffit of arch: Angels in roundel and Last Supper.* Lucca, S. Frediano. *About 1508–9.*

1721. ASPERTINI: *Fresco: The Volto Santo carried in procession from the sea into Lucca.* Detail.
Lucca, S. Frediano. *About 1508–9.*

1722. ASPERTINI: *Fresco: S. Frediano changes the course of the river Serchio.* Detail. Lucca, S. Frediano.
About 1508–9.

1723. ASPERTINI: *Fresco: S. Frediano changes the course of the river Serchio.* Detail.
Lucca, S. Frediano. *About 1508–9.*

1724. ASPERTINI: *Portrait of young man*. Mellerstain,
Earl of Haddington.

1725. ASPERTINI: *Bust of young man*. Frankfurt,
Staedel Institute.

1726. ASPERTINI: *Bust of old woman*. Homeless.

1727. ASPERTINI: *Bust of woman reading*. Baltimore,
Walters Art Gallery.

1729. Aspertini: *Madonna and Child with Saints.* Paris,
Saint-Nicolas-des-Champs.

1728. Aspertini: *Holy Family with female Saint.* Holkham, Earl of Leicester.

1731. MAZZOLINO: *Holy Family with S. Elizabeth and Infant S. John. Formerly Amsterdam, H. Tietje. Signed and dated 1511.*

1730. MAZZOLINO: *Detail of triptych: Madonna and Child. Berlin-Ost, Staatliche Museen. Dated 1509.*

1732. MAZZOLINO: *Nativity*. Formerly Paris, Bourgeois Collection.

1733. MAZZOLINO: *Adoration of the Magi*. Formerly Rome, Prince Ludovico Chigi della Rovere Albani.
Signed and dated 1512.

1734. MAZZOLINO: *Adoration of the Magi*. Formerly Easton Neston, Lord Hesketh. *Dated 1522.*

1736. MAZZOLINO: *Madonna and Child with S. Anthony Abbot.*
Chantilly, Musée Condé. *Dated 1526.*

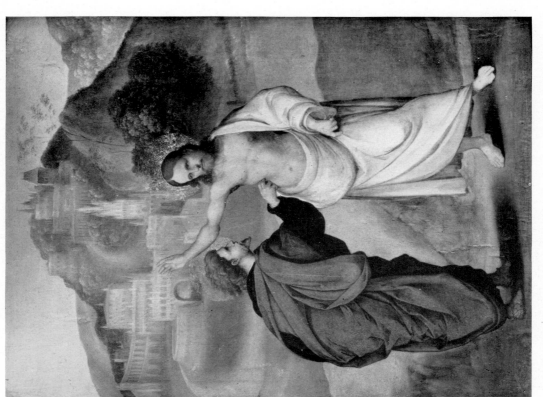

1735. MAZZOLINO: *Doubting Thomas.* Rome, Galleria Borghese.

1737. MAZZOLINO: *Pharaoh and his hosts overwhelmed in the Red Sea.* Dublin, National Gallery of Ireland.

1738. MAZZOLINO: *Christ driving the Money-changers from the Temple*. Alnwick, Duke of Northumberland. *Late work*.

1740. DOSSO: *The Baptist's head brought to Herod.* Homeless.
Early work.

1739. MAZZOLINO: *Christ and the Doctors.* Berlin-Ost, Staatliche Museen.
Signed and dated 1524.

1741. DOSSO: *One of ten Este panels with episodes from the Aeneid: Aeneas landing in Africa. Birmingham, Barber Institute. About 1520.*

1742. DOSSO: *One of ten Este panels with episodes from the Aeneid: Aeneas and the Cumaean Sibyl at the entrance of the Underworld. Ottawa, National Gallery of Canada. About 1520.*

1743. Dosso: *Adoration of the Magi*. London, National Gallery.

1744. DOSSO: *Youth with basket of flowers*. Florence, R. Longhi.

1745. DOSSO: *Poet and Muse*. Fragment. London, National Gallery.

1746. DOSSO: *S. Sebastian between S. John Baptist and S. Jerome, and above, the Madonna and Child between S. Lawrence and S. Roch.* Modena, Duomo. *1522.*

883

1748. Dosso: *Gentleman holding a letter*. Hampton Court, Royal Collection.

1747. Dosso: *General in armour*. Darmstadt, Landesgalerie.

1749. Dosso: *Jupiter, Mercury and Iris.* Vienna, Kunsthistorisches Museum.

1751. Dosso: *Allegory of Music*. Florence, Museo Horne.

1750. Dosso: *Young seated Prophet*. Tel Aviv, A. Rosner.

1752. Dosso: *Hercules and the Pygmies*. Graz, Landesmuseum Johanneum.

1753. RAPHAEL: *S. Michael*. Paris, Louvre.

1754. Dosso: *S. Michael*. Dresden, Gallery.

1755. DOSSO: *Temptation of Christ*. Homeless.

1756. DOSSO: *Holy Family with Infant S. John*. Homeless.

1757. Workshop of Dosso: *Flight into Egypt*. Coral Gables, Fla., Lowe Art Gallery, Kress Collection.

1758. Battista Dossi: *Flight into Egypt*. Formerly Leipzig, Fritz Harck.

1759. BATTISTA DOSSI: *Nativity*. Modena, Pinacoteca Estense. *1534*.

1760. Dosso and Battista Dossi: *Venus in landscape*. Formerly London, Donaldson Collection.
Late work.

1761. ORTOLANO: *Nativity*. Formerly Florence,
Loeser Collection.

1762. ORTOLANO: *Adoration of the Child
with Angels carrying Symbols of the Passion.*
Philadelphia, Johnson Collection.

1763. ORTOLANO: *Predella panel: Nativity*. Baltimore, Walters Art Gallery.

1764. ORTOLANO: *Detail from altarpiece: S. Demetrius*. London, National Gallery.

1765. Ortolano: *Christ and the Woman taken in adultery*. London, Courtauld Institute Galleries.

1766. Ortolano: *Circumcision and Saints*. Rome, Palazzo Patrizi.

1767. Ortolano: *S. John on Patmos*. Venice, Conte Vittorio Cini.

1768. ORTOLANO: *Crucifixion with S. John Baptist and Bishop Saint*. Milan, Brera.

1769. ORTOLANO: *Mourning over the dead Christ*. Naples, Galleria Nazionale di Capodimonte.
Signed and dated 1521.

1770. ORTOLANO: *Adoration of the Child with Infant S. John, S. Francis and S. Mary Magdalen.*
Rome, Galleria Doria Pamphili.

1771. ORTOLANO: *S. Margaret and the dragon*. Copenhagen, State Museum. *Dated 1524.*

1773. Ferrarese-Bolognese, 1450–1525 (close to early Garofalo): *Circumcision.* Homeless.

1772. Ferrarese-Bolognese, 1450–1525 (close to early Garofalo): *Madonna of the Monkey.* London, National Gallery.

1774. GAROFALO: *Nativity with Shepherd. Homeless. Early work.*

1775. GAROFALO: *Madonna and Child with SS. Eleucadius and Stephen*. Castellarano, S. Valentino.
Dated 1517.

1776. WORKSHOP OF GAROFALO: *Lunette: Flight into Egypt*. Ferrara, Pinacoteca. *1519*.

1777. GAROFALO: *Predella panel: Circumcision*. Paris, Louvre.

1778. GAROFALO: *Monochrome fresco: David.* Ferrara, Palazzo del Seminario. *1517–19.*

1779. GAROFALO: *Fresco: Ladies and gentlemen looking down*. Ferrara, Palazzo di Ludovico il Moro.

1780. GAROFALO: *Holy Family*. Frankfurt, Staedel Institute.

1781. GAROFALO: *Monochrome predella panel: S. Sylvester shows the picture of SS. Peter and Paul to the Emperor Constantine*. Ferrara, Pinacoteca.

1782. GAROFALO: *Adoration of the Shepherds.* London, Gordon Richardson.

1783. GAROFALO: *Marriage at Cana*. Leningrad, Hermitage. *Signed and dated 1531.*

1784. GAROFALO: *Vision of S. Augustine*. London, National Gallery.

1785. GAROFALO: *Madonna and Child with SS. Anne and Joachim*. Hampton Court, Royal Collection. *Signed and dated 1533.*

1786. GAROFALO: *Raising of Lazarus*. Ferrara, Pinacoteca. *Signed and dated 1534.*

1787. GAROFALO: *S. John Baptist taking leave of his father*. Bologna, S. Salvatore. *Signed and dated 1542.*

1788. CORREGGIO: *Nativity with S. Anne adoring the Child*. Milan, Brera. *Early work*.

1789. CORREGGIO: *Agony in the Garden*. London, Apsley House, Wellington Museum.

1790. CORREGGIO: *Marriage of S. Catherine*. Detroit, Institute of Arts. *Early work.*

1791. CORREGGIO: *Pietà*. Formerly Vienna,
Herrmann Eissler.

1792. CORREGGIO: *Madonna and Child with S. Joseph
in the background*. London, National Gallery.

1793. CORREGGIO: *Frescoed vault: Putti and allegories.* Parma, Convento di S. Paolo.

1796. CORREGGIO: *Rest during the Flight into Egypt, with Franciscan monk.*
Florence, Uffizi.

1797. CORREGGIO: *Martyrdom of SS. Placidus and Flavia.* Parma, Pinacoteca. *1520–4.*

1798. CORREGGIO: *Fresco: Vision of S. John Evangelist.* Detail. Parma, S. Giovanni Evangelista. *1524–30.*

1799. PARMIGIANINO: *Self-portrait in round mirror.*
Vienna, Kunsthistorisches Museum.

1800. PARMIGIANINO: *Holy Family.* London, Count Antoine Seilern.

1801. Parmigianino: *Galeazzo da San Vitale*. Naples, Galleria Nazionale di Capodimonte. *1524*.

1802. PARMIGIANINO: *Frescoes: Moses and canephora.* Parma, S. Maria della Steccata. *After 1531.*

1803. PARMIGIANINO: *Frescoes: Aaron and canephora.* Parma, S. Maria della Steccata. *After 1531.*

1804. PARMIGIANINO: *Fresco: Actaeon changed into a stag.* Fontanellato, Castello.

1806. PARMIGIANINO: *Fresco: Nymph pursued by Actaeon and a companion.*
Detail. Fontanellato, Castello.

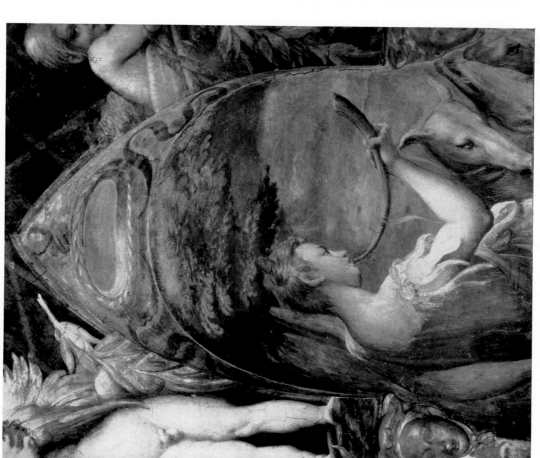

1805. PARMIGIANINO: *Fresco: Actaeon devoured by his dogs.* Detail.
Fontanellato, Castello.

1807. PARMIGIANINO: *Madonna and Child*. Rome, Galleria Doria Pamphili.

1808. PARMIGIANINO: *Portrait of a collector*. Formerly Wrotham Park, Earl of Strafford.

1809. Parmigianino: *Mystic Marriage of S. Catherine*. Somerley, Earl of Normanton.

1810. PARMIGIANINO: *Charles V and Victory*. Formerly Richmond, Cook Collection.

1811. GIROLAMO DA CARPI: *Archbishop Bartolini Salimbeni de' Medici.*
Florence, Palazzo Pitti.

1812. GIROLAMO DA CARPI: *Adoration of the Magi.* Modena, Galleria Estense.

1813. GIROLAMO DA CARPI: *Assumption of the Virgin with Giulia Muzzarella as donor.*
Washington, National Gallery of Art, Kress Collection.

1814–15. Girolamo da Carpi: *S. Luke and the Virgin*. London, Mrs. Gronau.—*Nativity*. London, Mr. and Mrs. J. A. Gere.

1816. GIROLAMO DA CARPI: *Holy Family with S. Catherine.* Glasgow, City Art Gallery.

1817. Girolamo da Carpi: *Judith*. Dresden, Gallery.

1818. Girolamo da Carpi: *Opportunity and Patience*. Dresden, Gallery. *1541.*

1818a. PERINO DEL VAGA: *Ornamental frescoes*. Pesaro, Villa Imperiale.

1819. PERINO DEL VAGA (ON RAPHAEL'S INDICATIONS): *Fresco: Joseph and his Brothers. Rome, Vatican, Logge di Raffaello. Completed 1519.*

1820. PERINO DEL VAGA: *Fresco: Jupiter destroys the Titans.* Genoa, Palazzo Doria, Sala dei Giganti.

1821. PERINO DEL VAGA: *Tondo: Holy Family*. Vaduz, Liechtenstein Collection.

1822–3. PERINO DEL VAGA: *Predella panels: Betrayal of Christ; Agony in the Garden*. Milan, Brera.
Signed. 1534.

1824. Perino del Vaga: *Nativity with SS. John Baptist, Sebastian, Roch, James, Catherine of Alexandria, and the Eternal*. Washington, National Gallery of Art, Kress Collection. *Signed and dated 1534.*

1825. PERINO DEL VAGA: *Frescoed frieze*. Rome, Palazzo Massimo alle Colonne.

1826. PERINO DEL VAGA: *Fresco: Scene from the Aeneid*. Rome, Palazzo Massimo alle Colonne.

1827. PERINO DEL VAGA: *Frescoed frieze*. Rome, Palazzo Massimo alle Colonne.

1828. PERINO DEL VAGA: *Monochrome fresco: Moses gives the Law to the Hebrews*. Rome, Vatican, Stanza della Segnatura.

1829. PERINO DEL VAGA AND ASSISTANTS: *Frescoed decoration*. Rome, Museo di Castel S. Angelo, Sala Paolina. *1545–7*.

1830. PERINO DEL VAGA AND PERUZZI: *Frescoed decoration*. Rome, Palazzo della Cancelleria. *Before 1521.*

1831–3. PERUZZI: *Frescoes: Constellation; Orpheus; Deucalion and Pyrrha.* Rome, Farnesina. *1511.*

1834. PERUZZI: *Fresco: Simulated loggia*. Rome, Farnesina, Salone delle Prospettive.

1835. PERUZZI: *Frescoes: Nativity, Adoration of the Magi, Flight into Egypt and six scenes from the Old Testament. Rome, S. Maria della Pace. Dated 1516.*

1837. PERUZZI: *Holy Family.* London, Philip Pouncey.

1836. PERUZZI: *Fresco: Madonna and Child with S. Catherine of Siena, S. Catherine of Alexandria and Ponzetti as donor.* Rome, S. Maria della Pace. *1516.*

1838. PERUZZI: *Cartoon for G. B. Bentivoglio's Adoration of the Magi.* London, National Gallery. *Signed. 1521.*

1839. PERUZZI: *Fresco: Playing putti.* Rome, Villa Madama.

1840. PERUZZI: *Ceiling fresco: Judgement of Paris.* Belcaro, Castello.

1841. GENGA: *Madonna suckling the Child, and Infant S. John.*
Formerly London, Sir Henry Haworth. *Early work.*

1842. GENGA: *Predella panel: S. Augustine giving the habit to three catechumens.*
Columbia, S.C., Museum of Art, Kress Collection. *1513–18.*

1843. GENGA: *Transfiguration*. Siena, S. Maria Assunta, Museo dell'Opera. *1510*.

1844. GENGA: *Madonna with the Holy Children, six Saints, four Fathers of the Church, three singing putti in foreground, and the Eternal above with putti scattering jasmin blossoms.* Milan, Brera. *1513–18.*

1845. GENGA: *Resurrection*. Rome, S. Caterina da Siena. *Signed*.

1846. GENGA: *Ceiling fresco: Francesco Maria della Rovere and his troops*. Pesaro, Villa Imperiale. *1530*.

1847. GENGA: *Detached fresco: Flight of Aeneas from Troy*. Siena, Pinacoteca. *1509–10*.

1848. GENGA: *Detached fresco: Freeing of prisoners.* Siena, Pinacoteca. *1509–10.*

1850. GIULIO ROMANO: *Holy Family with SS. James, Mark and Infant John.* Rome, S. Maria dell'Anima.

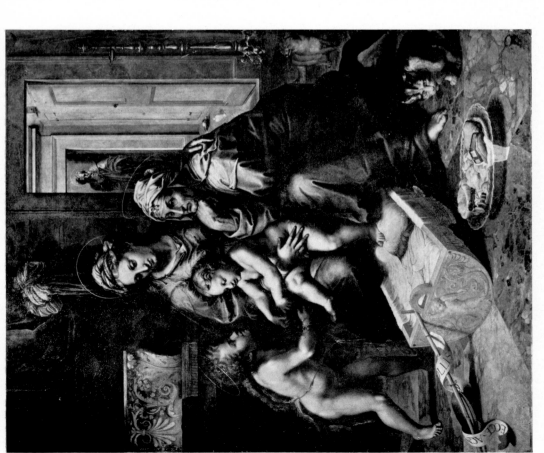

1849. GIULIO ROMANO: '*Madonna del gatto.*' Naples, Galleria Nazionale di Capodimonte.

1851. Giulio Romano: *Frescoes: Olympic Contests.* Rome, Villa Albani.

1852. GIULIO ROMANO: *Stoning of S. Stephen.* Genoa, S. Stefano. *About 1523.*

1853. GIULIO ROMANO: *Fresco: Battle of Ponte Molle*. Detail. Rome, Vatican, Sala di Costantino. *1524*.

1854. Giulio Romano: *Nativity*. Paris, Louvre. *1531*.

1855. GIULIO ROMANO AND ASSISTANTS: *Frescoes: Scenes from the Story of Cupid and Psyche.*
Mantua, Palazzo del Tè. *1532–4.*

1856. GIULIO ROMANO AND ASSISTANTS: *Frescoed walls.* Mantua, Palazzo del Te. *1532–4.*

1856a. GIOLFINO: *Fresco: View of Verona*. Detail from *S. Francis renouncing his inheritance*.
Verona, S. Bernardino. *About 1522*.

1857. LIBERALE DA VERONA: *Illuminated page: Descent of the Holy Ghost*. Verona, Museo di Castelvecchio.

1858. LIBERALE DA VERONA: *Madonna and Child enthroned with S. Lawrence, S. Christopher and two Olivetan Saints.* Berlin-Ost, Staatliche Museen. *Signed and dated 1489.*

1859. LIBERALE DA VERONA: *Virgin and Child in the lap of S. Anne*. Cracow, Museum.

1860. LIBERALE DA VERONA: *Sacrifice of Isaac with Francesco Miniscalchi and his sister as donors.*
Verona, Museo di Castelvecchio.

1861. LIBERALE DA VERONA: *Death of the Virgin.* Verona, Palazzo Arcivescovile.

1863. LIBERALE DA VERONA: *Fresco: Cherubim.* Detail of *Mourning over the dead Christ.* Verona, S. Anastasia.

1862. LIBERALE DA VERONA: *Adoration of the Magi.* Detail. Verona, S. Maria Matricolare.

1865. LIBERALE DA VERONA: *Dead Christ in sepulchre upheld by Angels.*
London, Philip Pouncey.

1864. LIBERALE DA VERONA: *Madonna and Child with four Angels.*
Stockholm, University Gallery.

1866. LIBERALE DA VERONA: *Detail of organ-shutter:*
Adoration of the Magi. Verona, Museo di Castelvecchio.

1867. TORBIDO: *Madonna and Child.*
Verona, Museo di Castelvecchio.

1868. TORBIDO: *S. Francis recommends the Conte Sanbonifacio to the Holy Family.*
Verona, Museo di Castelvecchio.

1869. TORBIDO: *Portrait of youth*. Munich, Alte Pinakothek. *Signed and dated 1516*.

1870. TORBIDO: *Bust of man with black hat*. Milan, Brera. *Signed*.

1871. TORBIDO: *Circumcision*. Messina, Museo.

1872. TORBIDO: *Madonna and Child in glory with Trinity above, Tobias and the Angel and S. Apollonia below.*
Verona, S. Fermo Maggiore. *Signed and dated 1523.*

1873. TORBIDO: *Mystic Marriage of S. Catherine, with Giacomo Fontanelli and his wife as S. James and S. Mary Magdalen*. Potsdam, Neues Palais. *Signed*.

1874. G. F. CAROTO: *Massacre of the Innocents*. Florence, Uffizi. *Signed*.

1875. G. F. Caroto: *Virgin sewing and Holy Children.*
Modena, Galleria Estense. *Signed and dated 1502.*

1876. G. F. Caroto: *Madonna and Child.*
Formerly Budapest, Sandor Lederer.

1877. G. F. Caroto: *Madonna adoring the Child.*
Leipzig, Museum.

1878. G. F. Caroto: *Madonna and Child.*
Frankfurt, Staedel Institute. *Signed. Early work.*

1879. G. F. CAROTO: *Detail of fresco: Virgin of the Annunciation*. Verona, S. Girolamo.
Signed and dated 1508.

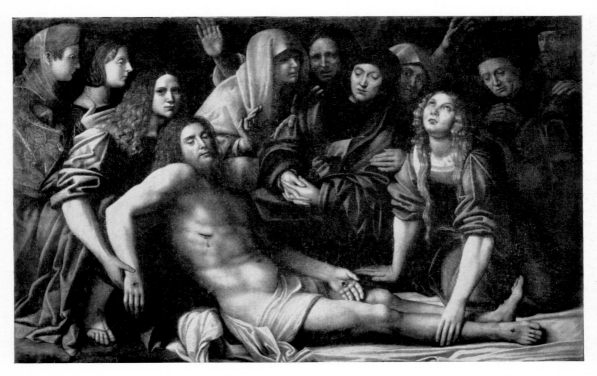

1880. G. F. CAROTO: *Mourning over the dead Christ*. Formerly Turin, Vincenzo Fontana.
Signed and dated 1515.

1881. G. F. CAROTO: *Detail of fresco: Caryatid.* Volargne, Villa Del Bene.

1882. G. F. CAROTO: *Predella panel: The Virgin laid on the bier.* London, Philip Pouncey.

1883. G. F. CAROTO: *Madonna and Child with butterfly*. Formerly Vienna, Baron Tucher. *Signed.*

1884. G. F. CAROTO: *Madonna and Child with youthful Baptist, S. Joseph and Holy Ghost.* Formerly Milan, Benigno Crespi. *Signed. About 1530.*

1885. G. F. CAROTO: *Predella panel: Birth of the Virgin*. Bergamo, Accademia Carrara. *Signed and dated 1527.*

1886. G. F. Caroto: *Holy Family with Infant S. John, S. Elizabeth and Angel.*
Verona, Museo del Castelvecchio. *Signed and dated 1531.*

1887. G. F. CAROTO: *Fresco: The sixth Trumpet Call of the Apocalypse.*
Volargne, Villa del Bene.

1888. G. F. CAROTO: *Predella panel: Mourning over the dead Christ.* Verona, S. Giorgio in Braida.

1889. G. F. Caroto: *Raising of Lazarus*. Verona, Palazzo Arcivescovile.
Signed and dated 1531.

1890. G. F. Caroto: *Predella panel: Agony in the Garden*. Verona, S. Giorgio in Braida.

1891. G. F. CAROTO AND GIOVANNI CAROTO: *Fresco: The Homecoming of Tobias with his bride and the Healing of his father.* Verona, S. Eufemia.

1892. GIOVANNI CAROTO: *Flight into Egypt.* Verona, Museo del Castelvecchio.

1893. GIOVANNI CAROTO: *Madonna and Child enthroned with SS. Martin and Stephen and donor.*
Verona, S. Maria Matricolare. *Signed and dated 1514.*

1894–5. GIOVANNI CAROTO: *Angel and Virgin of the Annunciation*. Verona, S. Giorgio in Braida.

1896. GIOVANNI CAROTO: *Madonna and Child enthroned with SS. Peter and Paul*. Verona, S. Paolo. *Signed and dated 1516.*

1897. GIOVANNI CAROTO: *Madonna and Child*. Formerly Brescia, Conti Martinengo.

1898. GIOVANNI CAROTO: *S. Ambrose between S. Paul and S. Joseph*. Detail. Verona, S. Maria della Scala.

1899. GIOVANNI CAROTO: *Madonna and Child appearing to SS. Andrew and Peter.* Verona, S. Stefano.
Late work.

1900. GIOLFINO: *Detached fresco: Astronomy*. Verona, Museo del Castelvecchio.

1901. GIOLFINO: *Cassone panel: Scene of dying youth*. Meggenhorn, Frau Baumann.

1902. GIOLFINO: *Detached fresco: War*. Verona, Museo del Castelvecchio.

1903. GIOLFINO: *Cassone panel: Scene of dying youth*. Meggenhorn, Frau Baumann.

1904. GIOLFINO: *Madonna and Child in landscape.*
Bergamo, Accademia Carrara.

1905. GIOLFINO: *Life of S. Julian.* Rome, Museo di Palazzo Venezia.

1906. GIOLFINO: *Madonna and Child in glory with Faith, Hope and Charity; below: SS. James and John Evangelist and donor*. Berlin-East, Staatliche Museen.

1907. GIOLFINO: *Christ in glory with Angels holding the Symbols of the Passion; below, S. Erasmus and S. George; in the background, Martyrdom of S. Erasmus; in the foreground, two donors of the Faella family.* Verona, S. Anastasia. *Signed and dated 1520.*

QVI HOMINVM MENTES PECCATORVM ACVLEIS SAVCIATAS MORIBVS ET DOCTRINA SANAVIT
ETIAM LOTVRA SACRARVM MANVVM XPI VEXILLA GERENTVM B FRANCISCVS BRVTIS
GRAVI MORBO LANGVENTIBVS PRAESTITIT MEDICINAM

1908. GIOLFINO: *Fresco: Scene from the life of S. Francis.* Verona, S. Bernardino. *About 1522.*

ANIMARVM SALVTEM B FRANCISCVS XPO CONFORMITER ZELANS INDVLGENTIAM ILLA
SACRAM AB IPSO MATRE VIRGINE INTERCEDENTE IMPETRAVIT ET A D HONORIO PP III ROSIS
HYEMALI TEMPORE COLLECTIS VERITATEM REI ATTESTANTIBVS CONFIRMARI CVRAVIT

1909. GIOLFINO: *Fresco: Scene from the life of S. Francis.* Verona, S. Bernardino. *About 1522.*

1910. GIOLFINO: *Lunette fresco: Ascension*. Verona, S. Maria in Organo.

1911–12. GIOLFINO: *Frescoes: Fall of manna; Jewish Passover.* Verona, S. Maria in Organo.

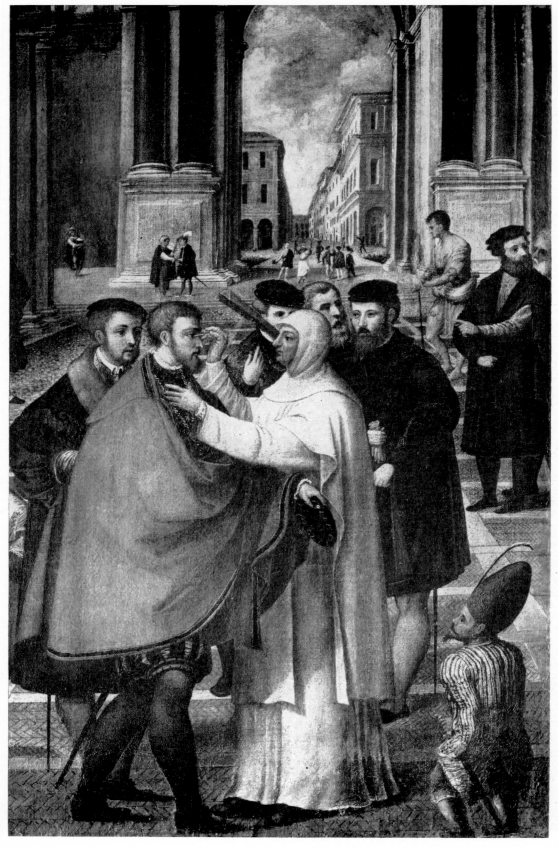

1913. BADILE: *Detail from the Circumcision*. Turin, Galleria Sabauda. *Early work*.

1914. BADILE: *Madonna and Child with SS. Peter, Andrew and John Evangelist.*
Verona, Museo del Castelvecchio. *Signed and dated 1544.*

1916. BADILE: *Madonna and Holy Children in glory;
below, SS. Scholastica, Benedict, Prosdocinus and Justina.*
Padua, Museo Civico. 1552.

1915. BADILE: *Raising of Lazarus.* Verona, S. Bernardino. *Dated 1546.*

1918. Farinati: *S. Mary Magdalen adoring the Cross.* Prague, National Gallery.

1917. Farinati: *S. Martin and the beggar.* Mantua, Duomo. 1552.

1919. FARINATI: *Frescoed lunette: Adam and Eve.* Verona, SS. Nazzaro e Celso. *1557.*

1920. FARINATI: *Fresco: Beheading of SS. Nazarus and Celsus.* Detail. Verona, SS. Nazzaro e Celso.

1921. FARINATI: *SS. Francis and Anthony of Padua worshipping the Eternal.*
Frassino, Santuario della Madonna. *Signed and dated 1560.*

1922. FARINATI: *Madonna appearing to SS. Francis and Sebastian and the Blessed Andrea Grego.*
Frassino, Santuario della Madonna. *Signed and dated 1576.*

1923. FARINATI: *Conversion of S. Paul*. Prun, Parish Church. *Signed and dated 1590.*

1925. Farinati: *Nativity*. Salò, S. Bernardino. *Signed and dated 1584.*

1924. Farinati: *Holy Family with S. Elizabeth and Infant S. John.*
Frassino, Santuario della Madonna. *Dated 1586.*

1926. FARINATI: Fresco: *Victory of the Veronese over Barbarossa at Vaccaldo.* Verona, Palazzo della Gran Guardia. *1598.*

1927. FARINATI: *The Council of Trent.* Paris, Louvre.

1929. FARINATI: *Mystic Marriage of S. Catherine. Pavia, Museo Malaspina.*

1928. FARINATI: *Christ on the way to Golgotha. Rome, Museo di Palazzo Venezia.*

1930. BRUSASORCI: *Detail of detached fresco: Spring.* Trent, Municipio. *1551.*

1931. BRUSASORCI: *Detail of detached fresco: Scene from Roman History.* Trent, Municipio. *1551.*

1932. BRUSASORCI: *Fresco: Conversion of S. Paul*. Verona, SS. Trinità.

1933. BRUSASORCI: *S. Margaret in prison*. Mantua, Duomo. *1552*.

1934. BRUSASORCI: *Man with white beard.*
Baltimore, Walters Art Gallery.

1935. BRUSASORCI: *Prelate.* Formerly Bergamo,
Alma and Maria Frizzoni. Destroyed.

1936. BRUSASORCI: *Shepherd and flock.*
Philadelphia, John G. Johnson Collection.

1937. BRUSASORCI: *Male portrait.*
Milan, Castello Sforzesco.

1938. BRUSASORCI: *The Man possessed by the Devil, and two allegorical figures.* Verona, S. Giorgio in Braida.

1939. BRUSASORCI: *Fresco: Two caryatids and landscape with Biblical scene.* Volargne, Villa del Bene.

1940. BRUSASORCI: *Fresco: Caryatids and landscape with Biblical scene*. Volargne, Villa del Bene.

1941–2. BRUSASORCI: *Two cupboard doors: Temptation of Christ and Parable of the Field of Wheat. Verona, S. Maria in Organo.*

1943. BRUSASORCI: *Detail of fresco: Entry of Charles V and Pope Clement VII into Bologna.* Verona, Palazzo Ridolfi da Lisca.

1944. BRUSASORCI: *Fresco: Landscape*. Verona, Palazzo Arcivescovile. *1566.*

1945. BRUSASORCI: *Fresco: Landscape*. Verona, Palazzo Arcivescovile. *1566.*

1945a. GIULIO CAMPI: *Detached fresco: Fragment of frieze*. Brescia, Pinacoteca. *Late work.*

1946. GIULIO CAMPI: *Madonna and Child with SS. Nazzarus and Celsus*. Cremona, S. Abbondio.
Signed and dated 1527.

1947. GIULIO CAMPI: *Allegory*. Milan, Museo Poldi Pezzoli.
Signed and dated 152(1?).

1948. GIULIO CAMPI: *Nativity with S. Francis and two donors*. Detail. Milan, Brera.

1949. GIULIO CAMPI: *Detail of frescoed vault: S. Luke*. Soncino, S. Maria delle Grazie. *1530*.

1950. GIULIO CAMPI: *Detail of fresco: Burial of S. Agatha*. Cremona, S. Agata. *Signed and dated 1537*.

1951. GIULIO CAMPI: *Young woman arranging flowers in a vase.*
Formerly Milan, Marchese Fossati.

1952. GIULIO CAMPI: *SS. Daria, Sigismund, Jerome and Chrysanthes recommend Francesco and Bianca Sforza to the Madonna and Child.* Detail. Cremona, S. Sigismondo. *Signed and dated 1540.*

1953. GIULIO CAMPI: *Frescoes: Judgement of Solomon; S. Augustine; and other scenes.* Cremona,
S. Sigismondo. *1542.*

1954. GIULIO CAMPI: *Fresco: Circumcision*. Cremona, S. Margherita. *1547.*

1955. GIULIO CAMPI: *Last Supper*. Detail. Cremona, Duomo. *Signed.*

1956. GIULIO CAMPI: *Man with glove*. Homeless.

1957. GIULIO CAMPI: *Man with black cap*. Hampton Court. Royal Collection.

1958. GIULIO CAMPI: *Baptism of Christ*. Cremona, Duomo. *Signed. 1568.*

1959. G. B. Moroni: *Gian Girolamo Grumelli*. Bergamo, Conte Moroni. *Signed and dated 1560.*

1960. G. B. MORONI: *Lucia Vertova*. Nantes, Musée.

1961. G. B. MORONI: *Monk*. Rotterdam, Museum Boymans–Van Beuningen.

1962. G. B. MORONI: *Profile of donor contemplating Baptism of Christ*. Genoa, Basevi Collection.

1963. G. B. MORONI: *Last Supper*. Romano Lombardo, S. Maria Assunta. *1568*.

1964. G. B. Moroni: *Conte Ercole Tassi*. Milan, Castello Sforzesco.

1965. G. B. MORONI: *S. George and the dragon*. Gazzaniga, S. Giorgio a Fiorano. *1575*.

1966. G. B. Moroni: *Portrait of a widower with his sons*. Dublin, National Gallery of Ireland.

1967. ANGUISSOLA: *Self-portrait at the easel*. Keir, Lt. Col. William Stirling.

1968. ANGUISSOLA: *The three sisters and the governess of the artist*. Poznan, National Museum.
Signed and dated 1555.

1969. ANGUISSOLA: *Holy Family with Infant S. John and S. Francis.* Formerly Milan, Cavalieri Collection. *Signed.*

1971. ANGUISSOLA: *Dominican astronomer.* Formerly Terzo d'Aquileja, Calligaris Collection. *Signed and dated* 155(5?).

1970. ANGUISSOLA: *Don Giulio Clovio seated at a table.* Rome, Mentana, Federico Zeri.

1973. ANGUISSOLA: *Self-portrait at the harpsichord, with an old woman looking on.* Althorp, Earl Spencer. *Signed and dated 1561.*

1972. ANGUISSOLA: *Bearded old man seated at a table, with his left hand on an open book.* Burghley House, Marquess of Exeter. *Signed.*

1974. ANGUISSOLA: *Self-portrait in medallion.* Paris, Frits Lugt.
Signed and dated 1558.

1975. ANGUISSOLA: *Portrait of an old woman.*
Nivaagaard, Hage Collection.

1976. ANGUISSOLA: *Boy with sword, gloves and dog*. Baltimore, Walters Art Gallery.

1977. SCARSELLINO: *Susanna and the Elders*. Philadelphia, John G. Johnson Collection. *Early work.*

1978. SCARSELLINO: *Vision of the dying Magdalen in the wilderness*. Ferrara, S. Domenico.

1979. SCARSELLINO: *Holy Family with Infant S. John.*
Bologna, F. Molinari Pradelli. *Early work.*

1980. SCARSELLINO: *Madonna and Child
with Infant S. John.* Homeless.

1981. SCARSELLINO: *Venus and Endymion.* Rome, Galleria Borghese.

1982. SCARSELLINO: *Assumption of Enoch*. Rome, Galleria Pallavicini.

1983. SCARSELLINO: *Madonna and Child with Infant S. John*. Burghley House, Marquess of Exeter.

1984. SCARSELLINO: *Flight into Egypt*. Rome, Pinacoteca Capitolina.

1985. SCARSELLINO: *Adoration of the Magi*. Formerly Linlathen, Col. Erskine.

1986. SCARSELLINO: *Vision of S. Francis*. Formerly Rome,
Galleria Barberini.

1987. SCARSELLINO: *Christ and the plague-stricken*. Homeless.

1988. SCARSELLINO: *Holy Family with S. Barbara and S. Carlo Borromeo.* Dresden, Gallery. *1615.*

DATE DUE